SPORTS GOVERNANCE

Anne McFarland

SPORTS GOVERNANCE

A Guide for Sporting Entities

Anne McFarland

ORPEN PRESS

Published by
Orpen Press
Upper Floor, Unit B3
Hume Centre
Hume Avenue
Park West Industrial Estate
Dublin 12
Ireland

email: info@orpenpress.com
www.orpenpress.com

Paperback ISBN 978-1-78605-093-9
ePub ISBN 978-1-78605-094-6

Printed in Dublin by SPRINTprint Ltd

'The most important thing in the Olympic Games is not winning but taking part; the essential thing in life is not conquering but fighting well.'

Pierre de Coubertin
(founder of the modern Olympic Games)

Dedicated to all in sport who 'fight well'.

FOREWORD

Governance is not a destination but a journey, one that all sporting bodies are on. This journey requires focus and scrutiny to ensure both forward-looking progress and rear-view monitoring. The journey can be complex. The environment in which we operate is constantly changing and throws up new challenges. The purpose of this book is to guide us and our organisations along the road of good governance.

In sport possibly the greatest challenge is ensuring that the right level of decision-making occurs at the appropriate level within the organisation. It is also important that these decisions are communicated and monitored. Defining what decision-making is reserved for the board, where else decision-making occurs and what they as a board will monitor is also key. For it is the board that sets the framework for the good governance of an organisation.

Governance of a sporting entity is not about ticking boxes but is about creating a culture that allows the sport to flourish and succeed. It is about getting individuals on the board who have the time commitment, dedication and ability to put the organisation before their club/regional or other needs, and the will to succeed.

It is about getting the board to think strategically as to what they want to achieve and how they plan to achieve it.

It is about the board supporting and challenging the executive.

It is about making sure that the board members know their role and their legal duties and ensuring that training and evaluation of board members is ongoing.

It is about ongoing integrity in decision-making. In short, it is a continuous journey that never stops.

This book takes us along that journey, starting with an introduction to governance and the structure of sport in Ireland. It then looks at what becoming a board member means and finally considers the key functions of a board – strategy, risk, accountability and monitoring.

At the Olympic Federation of Ireland, good governance has been a particular area of focus for the organisation. We are proud to support this book by Anne McFarland, which we hope will be a resource to all sports and governing bodies, ourselves included.

Anne McFarland is uniquely qualified to author such a book. She recently co-authored *A Practical Guide to Corporate Governance*, a detailed guide extensively cross-referenced to the Companies Act 2014. She is a chartered accountant who lectures regularly on governance and ethics. However, it is her passion for sport, and in particular governance in sport, that led her to write this book. It is written not for accountants or governance specialists, but for those of us who are actually involved in administering sport at no matter what level. It is not only directed at the larger organisation but also at smaller entities, such as clubs or regional organisations. Each chapter includes a useful summary of the issues for the smaller entity as well as ten key points to remember.

Personally I found the chapter on accountability and ethics of particular interest. Ethics must start from the top of the organisation, instilling key values in its culture. It is so important to understand the environment in which you are operating and to manage the integrity of your organisation.

Irish athletes want to be the best in the world. We also want sport to be inclusive and to give everyone a chance. To achieve this all of us who are involved in governing sport must dedicate ourselves to making sure that our sporting entities are running as effectively as possible.

In this book Anne shows us an excellent road map. It is up to each of us to undertake the journey.

Sarah Keane
President
Olympic Federation of Ireland

PREFACE

The National Sports Policy requires Sport Ireland to ensure that all bodies it funds have adopted a code of governance by the end of 2021. The specific code of governance required is the Governance Code for the Community, Voluntary and Charity Sector (henceforward referred to as the Sports Code). As part of this process, Sport Ireland will identify and put in place the training and supports needed by different organisations to assist with the adoption process.[1]

This is a very welcome development. Sport Ireland has been working closely with the governing bodies of individual sports to ensure that they run their sport to a good standard of governance. While most national governing bodies are professionally staffed, the majority of sporting entities, e.g. clubs and leagues, may be run entirely by volunteers. Many board members have a profound knowledge of the sport but they may not have experience in governance. Some may not even know whether their entity is a company or not. They may consider that the Companies Act is for their legal advisors, the financial statements are for their accountant to prepare, and governance means ticking a few boxes.

The scandals that have been seen in the voluntary and charity sector have turned the focus to governance. Sport too must be run according to best accepted practice. Neither the government, sponsors nor the public are willing to condone a relaxed approach to governance. All sporting entities must be run efficiently and effectively, in a professional manner. Just because a sporting entity is largely manned by volunteers does not mean that it cannot be run professionally by them.

The task is challenging. Play the Game, an organisation that monitors governance in international sports federations, concluded in 2015 that most sports federations are in need of fundamental reform:

> 'Among the most important findings ... are that the great majority of the sports federations have no term limits on elected officials, no public information on accounts and activities, no integrity checks of their leaders, no insight into salaries and perks and no effective internal control mechanisms such as independent ethics and audit committees.'[2]

This book draws on the Sports Code as well as on the Companies Act 2014. The aim is to guide the board member of a sporting entity as to their role. It looks at what steps should be considered when deliberating whether to become a board member. It sets out what board members need to know to comply with the Sports Code and looks at some practical issues of implementation. Governance is not difficult. Much of it is common sense.

This book looks at what is required for larger organisations to illustrate best practice, but each chapter concludes with a list of recommendations for the smaller entity.

The book draws on my practical experience as a financial board member and as an advisor on governance as well as my interest in sport, both amateur and professional. I believe that the introduction of the Sports Code by Sport Ireland for all funded bodies is an excellent step in improving sports governance. The next step is to ensure that adequate training is put in place for board members and the executive and that governance filters down to all sporting entities.

The book is set out in three parts:

- Part I: An Introduction to Governance. This is a single chapter which outlines the organisation of sport in Ireland and then discusses the rationale for better governance in sport.
- Part II: Becoming a Board Member looks at the importance of investigating an organisation before becoming a board member as well as the different roles on a board, the running of meetings, and development and evaluation of the board.
- Part III: The Board – Strategy, Risk, Accountability and Monitoring deals with the key functions of a board, emphasising the importance of a clear strategy and an understanding of risk. It touches on the accountability of the board and ethics as well as the key area, particularly for larger entities, of monitoring the performance of the entity and in particular that of the executive.

There is an extensive index allowing the reader, if they wish, to use the book as a reference. Each chapter is self-sufficient with an introduction and conclusion as well as ten key points to remember. In addition, for each chapter there is a summary of points for the smaller entity, which is referenced to the Sports Code. For ease of reference, particularly for those in clubs that may be unaware of the Sports Code, the Sports Code for smaller entities, called Type A, is included as an appendix. For those in larger entities with employees (Type B organisations) or for large sporting entities (Type C organisations), the Sports Code can be accessed currently at https://www.governancecode.ie/the-code.html.

For those who aim to understand governance in a sporting entity this book is a practical guide. It starts with the question – what is governance?

ACKNOWLEDGEMENTS

I would like to thank sincerely the following for their contributions:

The Olympic Federation of Ireland for its support in my publishing a book focusing on governance. Governance is now recognised as a core foundation of the work it is doing as a sporting organisation. The Federation's support was an invaluable part of bringing this book to fruition.

Sarah O'Shea of SOS Sports Consult, a consultant working with sporting bodies in the area of governance and the Honorary General Secretary of the Olympic Federation of Ireland, for her input into and review of each chapter of this book and her overall support in bringing this to life.

Dr Tom Courtney, leading practitioner and author in company law, and partner and head of the Company Compliance and Governance practice in Arthur Cox for his input and review as I wrote this book. Dr Courtney has been the chairperson of the Company Law Review Group, CLRG, which drafted the heads of bill, and on whose recommendations the innovations of the Companies Act are based.

Kate Hills, National Children's Officer Swim Ireland, for her specific review of the Safeguarding Children section.

Caroline Corballis for her energy in reading and re-reading drafts.

CONTENTS

Foreword vii
Preface... xi
Acknowledgements... xiv
Author's Note xix

Part I: Introduction To Governance.......................... 1

1. What Is Governance?... 3
   Introduction.. 3
   Background: The Organisation of Sport in Ireland 4
   What Is Governance? 7
   The Sports Code.. 9
   The Need for a Governance Code in Sporting Entities .. 11
   The Smaller Entity 15
   Conclusion 15

Part II: Becoming A Board Member 19

2. Before Joining a Board 21
   Introduction 22
   Investigating the Organisation 22
   Board Members' Duties... 29

The Chair.. 30
The Company Secretary.. 31
Independent Board Members 31
Types of Board Member 33
Trustees 34
The Smaller Entity 35
Conclusion 36

3. On Joining the Board... 38
Introduction 38
Induction... 39
Matters Reserved for the Board.................................... 49
The Board as Leader 51
Committees 52
The Smaller Entity 57
Conclusion 58

4. First Meeting as a Board Member................................ 61
Introduction 62
How Meetings Should Be Run 62
The Role of the Chair in Meetings................................. 68
Updates on Activities 69
After the Meeting 72
Culture.. 73
The Smaller Entity 74
Conclusion 75

5. Board Member Activities 76
Introduction 76
Recruitment and Succession... 77
Development and Evaluation of the Board 81
Board Size 83
Length of Service – Board Members 83
Leaving the Board... 84
The Smaller Entity 84
Conclusion 85

Part III: The Board – Strategy, Risk, Accountability, Monitoring **87**

6. Strategy 89
   Introduction... 90
   The Need for a Strategy................................. 90
   The Constitution 91
   Vision and Mission... 92
   The Strategic Plan.. 93
   Budgets.. 98
   Measuring Success and Key Performance Indicators......... 99
   Stakeholders and External Influencers.............. 100
   The Smaller Entity 103
   Conclusion 104

7. Risk 106
   Introduction... 107
   Understanding Risk Management..................... 107
   Understanding the Accounts 111
   Systems and Controls...................................... 114
   Role of the External Auditor 117
   Role of Internal Auditors and the Audit Committee 119
   Insurance.. 121
   Risks Associated with Not Incorporating......... 125
   Disaster Recovery/Continuity Plans 126
   The Smaller Entity... 128
   Conclusion 128

8. Accountability 131
   Introduction... 132
   Accounting to Stakeholders........................... 132
   General Meetings 135
   Expenses Policy 138
   Gifts and Donations 139
   Conflicts of Interest and Loyalty 140
   Board Members as Champions of the Organisation 141

Board Confidentiality 141
Being Ethical... 142
The Smaller Entity 144
Conclusion 146

9. Monitoring 148
Introduction 149
The CEO – Role and Responsibilities.................................... 149
People Issues... 150
Safeguarding Children and Young People 159
Company Law.. 163
Tax.. 164
Financial Obligations 165
Integrity of Sport... 168
The Smaller Entity 172
Conclusion 173

Appendix.. 176
Introduction to the Sports Code Type A............................. 176
Principle 1: Leading Our Organisation 177
Principle 2: Exercising Control Over Our Organisation.. 178
Principle 3: Being Transparent and Accountable 179
Principle 4: Working Effectively.. 180
Principle 5: Behaving with Integrity....................................... 182

Endnotes 183
References.. 192
Index 198

Author's Note

This book uses the terms 'board' and 'board member' instead of 'governing body' and 'member of the governing board' respectively. The term 'board member' is specifically used to describe a board member of a company. If the organisation is not a company, it will not have board members. In this case, the words refer to the management committee, coordinating committee, governing body, trustees, committee core group or other relevant structure which makes the final decisions in the organisation. The practices stay the same.

Similarly, the word 'constitution' is used to cover any founding document setting out why the entity exists and how it should be run.

The 'executive' is used to describe those who are running the sport day-to-day. They may be volunteers, employees or consultants. In a smaller entity the executive and the board are likely to be one entity.

The term 'sporting entity' is used to describe all entities involved in the running of sport, including international federations, national governing bodies, local sports partnerships, clubs and affiliated bodies.

The word 'chair' covers president, where there is a president.

References to the Sports Code refer to the Governance Code for Community, Voluntary and Charitable Organisations (CVC Code) which was launched in 2012. It became the standard for governance in non-profit organisations. It was developed and maintained by the Governance Code Working Group.

Sport Ireland took the code over as the Governance Code for Sport (the Sports Code) in June 2019.[3] References in the endnotes such as 'Principle 3.2a of the Sports Code' are to the Sports Code. The Sports Code covers three types of organisations: Types A, B and C. Type A organisations are for smaller sporting entities. Type B relates to medium-sized entities or organisations that have employees. Type C relates to larger organisations. The Sports Code for Type A bodies is provided at the end of this book. Type B and C organisations have some additional requirements. If your organisation is a Type B or C entity you can find the relevant Sports Code for your organisation at www.governancecode.ie/the-code.html.

PART I

INTRODUCTION TO GOVERNANCE

1

WHAT IS GOVERNANCE?

- Introduction
- Background: The Organisation of Sport in Ireland
- What Is Governance?
- The Sports Code
- The Need for a Governance Code in Sporting Entities
- The Smaller Entity
- Conclusion
- Ten Key Points

INTRODUCTION

This chapter looks at the organisation of sport in Ireland and reflects why sporting entities are being asked to implement a code of governance. The particular code of governance which the Minister for Sport, together with Sport Ireland, selected for the sports sector is the Governance Code for Community, Voluntary and Charitable Organisations, now renamed the Sports Code.

BACKGROUND: THE ORGANISATION OF SPORT IN IRELAND

To set the context for a guide to governance in sport in Ireland it is worth considering the main entities associated with running sport in Ireland.

Department of Transport, Tourism and Sport

The Department of Transport, Tourism and Sport aims to:

- 'increase participation and interest in sport at all levels
- improve standards of performance and to develop sports facilities at national, regional and local level.'[4]

The department developed the National Sports Policy 2018–2027 with specific targets, including:

- Increasing participation to 50% of the population
- High-performance funding to deliver more Olympic and Paralympic medals
- The adoption by all funded sports bodies of the Sports Code

Sport Ireland and the National Governing Bodies

Established under the Sport Ireland Act 2015, Sport Ireland (previously the Irish Sports Council, established 1999), is the statutory body responsible for planning, leading and coordinating the sustainable development of competitive and recreational sport in Ireland.

National Governing Bodies (NGBs)

Sport Ireland works in partnership with the national governing bodies of sport (NGBs) to deliver sport to the Irish community. Notwithstanding this, all national governing bodies are independent, autonomous entities and are responsible for the governance and administration of their sports.

Sport Ireland has developed a set of recognition criteria should an organisation wish to become a 'Sport Ireland recognised National Governing Body of Sport'. These include:

- Governance
- Leadership
- Organisational structure
- Financial management
- Compliance

NGBs, where relevant, are mandated by their international federation. They may also have a European federation to which they are accountable. The international federation is responsible for setting regulations for membership and affiliation, and rules and regulations for each sport. Where the NGB represents an Olympic sport, the NGB is also subject to the Olympic Federation of Ireland or Paralympics Ireland in relation to the games.

Local Sports Partnerships

Sport Ireland works in partnership with local sports partnerships (LSPs),[5] whose aim is to increase participation in sport in the community through education, the development of clubs, and projects particularly aimed at specific target groups such as older people, women and girls, people with disabilities, unemployed people, and those who live in disadvantaged communities.

The Olympic Federation of Ireland (formerly the Olympic Council of Ireland)

The Olympic Federation of Ireland (OFI) is the mandated member of the International Olympic Movement for Ireland. It is required to comply with the rules both of the International Olympic

Committee and also the European Olympic Committee. The OFI works to improve the Olympic performance of Irish athletes in each Olympic cycle and inspire the nation through the success of our Olympic athletes.

To do this, it fosters a culture of performance in partnership with its stakeholders. It provides practical, effective support to add value to the NGBs, and uses the power of sport as a cause for good in Ireland.

It is responsible for supporting the development of sport in Ireland and selects teams for Olympics subject to international federations' qualifying guidelines.

The Olympic Committee of Ireland, after the Rio crisis, went through a substantial restructuring and overhauled its governance. Subsequently, it rebranded itself as the Olympic Federation of Ireland and set a new strategic plan.

Paralympics Ireland

Paralympics Ireland is the National Paralympic Committee for Ireland, recognised by the International Paralympic Committee and is the umbrella body of sporting organisations in Ireland providing programmes in sports on the Paralympic Games programme.

Federation of Irish Sport

The Federation of Irish Sport is an umbrella body for sports entities. It works to encourage NGBs and LSPs to liaise and work together to lobby on issues that affect sport. It describes itself as 'The Voice of Irish Sport'.

Sport Dispute Solutions Ireland (formerly Just Sport Ireland)

Sport Dispute Solutions Ireland (SDSI) aims to ensure that sporting disputes are heard in an appropriate setting rather than in the courts. It offers both mediation, where it tries to assist the disputing parties to come to a solution, and arbitration, where the parties agree to submit to the judgement of SDSI. Sport Ireland ask all NGBs to include SDSI as their appeals body unless they have a fully operational appeals body internally (e.g. FAI, IRFU, GAA).

SDSI can deal with all disputes that arise in a sporting context except for anti-doping and employment disputes.

Northern Ireland

Most sports are all-Ireland-based, with a few exceptions, notably soccer and sailing. Northern Ireland can send teams to the Commonwealth Games. Subject to each sport's eligibility requirements, an athlete from Northern Ireland may represent either Ireland or Great Britain in international competition.

The issue of eligibility has been tested at the Court of Arbitration for Sport, for instance when footballer Daniel Kearns' right to play for either territory was recognised.

Northern Ireland has a separate Sports Governance Code.[6]

The National Sports Policy 2018–2027 recognises the need to consider 'the challenge around "all-island" sports versus sports which operate on a jurisdictional basis'.[7]

Sport Northern Ireland

Sport Northern Ireland is the leading public body for the development of sport in Northern Ireland. It is a non-departmental public body funded by the Northern Ireland Exchequer and UK National Lottery. It recognises 83 sports, governed on an all-Ireland, UK or Northern Ireland-only basis, and works with its partners and stakeholders to deliver on its mission: 'To lead sports development at all levels, producing more participants and more winners.'[8]

WHAT IS GOVERNANCE?

Governance simply means governing an entity or directing it.

The phrase 'corporate governance' is sometimes used. This refers to when an entity is incorporated, i.e. it is a company.

The Cadbury Committee, headed by Sir Adrian Cadbury, who is seen today as the father of governance, gave what is perhaps the best-known definition of corporate governance, being:

'the system by which companies are directed and controlled'[9]

(Incidentally, Sir Adrian Cadbury was a sportsman, rowing in Great Britain's coxless four in the 1952 Summer Olympics in Helsinki.)

Sports bodies are either incorporated or unincorporated. Being incorporated means the sporting entity is registered in the Companies Registration Office (the CRO) as a company and has a board of directors, referred to in this book as 'board members'. An unincorporated entity is not a company. Unincorporated entities may operate in a variety of structures, the simplest and by far the most common being a committee structure. Even the simplest unincorporated entity has rules. There may be a constitution, a founding document or a rulebook setting out how that entity should be governed.

Historically, most sporting organisations in Ireland were formed as members' clubs and run by a committee. As the legal and business environment becomes more formalised and stringent, many sporting organisations are moving from an unincorporated structure to an incorporated structure. However, a weakness of these new companies is that they may not have implemented the policies and procedures to underpin their new structure. Often the existing committee members merely become board members without any knowledge of their role and legal responsibilities as company board members. Sometimes the election and appointment of such board members continues as before as if they were still committee members.

Board members of a sporting entity may have a profound and valuable knowledge of the sport, but do they know how to govern the entity effectively? Do they know under what rules they are directing it, what type of entity they are, what their constitution says? The constitution sets out the rules, but many board members of sporting organisations believe they can govern the entity unaware of the rules. Would they play a sport not knowing the rules?

To ensure that sporting entities are run well, each and every board member of a sporting entity must understand their duties under the Companies Act, if applicable, and the principles of the Sports Code. A lack of knowledge can result in inefficient systems, abuse of power and, at worst, personal liability of the board members.

Governance is not about well-meaning announcements by the chair and statements in the annual report or on the website. It is about actively regulating the relationships between the board members, the executive, the members and stakeholders of the sport. It is about directing and controlling the sporting entity.

THE SPORTS CODE

There are several codes of governance relating to different sectors. For instance, there is one for state bodies, one for public companies, and one for charities. The code that applies to most* sporting entities is 'The Governance Code for Community, Voluntary and Charitable Organisations in Ireland', referred to henceforth as the Sports Code. In line with the National Sports Policy, each entity funded by Sport Ireland needs to confirm that it is fully compliant with the Sports Code by the end of 2021. This confirmation must be independently verified.

The Sports Code is not law. It is simply a culmination of thinking as to how best to govern a sporting entity. It has three versions, depending on the size of the organisation. There is a simpler version for smaller sports, described as Type A organisations. Type B relates to medium-sized entities or organisations that have employees. Type C relates to larger organisations.

It is not a set of rules but a set of principles and recommended practice. The board may choose not to follow a certain

---

* There are some specific sporting exceptions, e.g. Horse Racing Ireland is subject to the Governance Code for State Bodies.

recommended practice, but it must explain why it chose that path and how it complies with the principles of the Sports Code.

The five principles of the Sports Code are:

- Leading the organisation
- Exercising control over the organisation
- Being transparent and accountable
- Working effectively
- Behaving with integrity

When Sport Ireland took over responsibility for the Sports Code in June 2019, the chair of Sport Ireland, Kieran Mulvey, said:

'This is an important step for Sport Ireland, which has a long history with the Code, having been the first state body to adopt the Code as best practice for our sector in 2013. In taking over the Code, Sport Ireland is reaffirming its commitment to supporting all funded bodies in putting in place and maintaining robust corporate governance structures.'[10]

UK Sport's 'A Code for Sports Governance'

UK Sport also has a specific code of governance for sport, 'A Code for Sports Governance'. Its key focus is on:

- Structure – clear and appropriate
- People – diverse, independent, experienced
- Communication – transparency and accountability
- Standards and Conduct – integrity
- Policies and Processes – compliance with all regulations and laws, financial planning and risk management

It emphasises the need for diverse, independent and experienced decision-makers.[11]

THE NEED FOR A GOVERNANCE CODE IN SPORTING ENTITIES

Poor Governance in Sporting Entities

Poor governance in sporting entities has been widely reported in recent years, with controversies causing serious reputational damage to numerous international federations, notably football, cycling, tennis and boxing. In Ireland too, the controversies that rocked the Football Association of Ireland (FAI) and the Olympic Council of Ireland have had significant repercussions.

Common causes of poor governance of sporting organisations include:

- Unfettered power by one or a small group of individuals
- A board member or individual putting their personal interest ahead of that of the members
- Lack of relevant skills held among board members
- Lack of financial understanding among board members
- Poor appreciation of risk among board members
- Unwieldy board and committee sizes
- Poor dissemination of information to members and stakeholders
- Absence of term limits for board members or chairs
- Lack of understanding of or reference to the constitution or rules of the entity
- Lack of checks and challenges
- Insular thinking and no external oversight
- Rare whistleblowing

The flow of money into sport is increasing. Commercialisation of sport brings added pressures. Even a small sport, with few physical spectators, if televised, may generate huge betting revenue, particularly abroad.

Unfortunately, within NGB affiliates and clubs there may be considerable resistance to running a sports club in an effective, professional manner. The board members of sporting organisations may prefer to focus not on governance but on the sport itself. Members stand by the innocence of sport and resist governance as merely ticking boxes, or as an exercise appropriate to business, or perhaps they see it as a waste of time – time which they believe needs to be spent discussing the sport. The inexperience of the board members, their failure to manage risk, their lack of understanding and implementation of financial controls, poor systems, lack of policies and poor reporting all contribute to poor governance. In particular, conflicts of interest remain an all too common and significant risk to good governance.

The Demand for Governance in Sport

It is time for participants, volunteers, fans, sponsors, promoters and board members to demand that sporting entities are run efficiently and effectively. Governance of sports and the rules and responsibilities of board members are becoming increasingly complex. The Sports Code is there to help them direct and control their organisation.

In June 2018, when Sport Ireland took over responsibility for the Sports Code, John Treacy, CEO of Sport Ireland, announced:

'Sport Ireland places a high premium on good governance, and encourages high standards in governance from all funded bodies. As a development agency, it is our aim to provide leadership in this area, empowering sport organisations to take responsibility for their own governance and meet the challenges that they face. In line with the actions laid out in the Government's National Sports Policy, Sport Ireland is looking forward to taking over the Code with a view to all funded bodies completing the adoption journey by 2021. To support this, we will continue to identify and put in place the training and supports needed by the different organisations to assist with the adoption process.'[12]

The Sports Code will be mandatory for all government-funded bodies. It is hoped that national governing bodies will encourage governance to filter down to club and league level although there is no requirement, other than the desire for good governance, for non-government-funded sporting entities to comply.

In short, sports need to be run in a professional manner. Even where the board members are volunteers there is no excuse for poor governance. In a sport, they are managing not only the funds but also the hopes and dreams of their members. The board is responsible for running the entity, so if it really wants to run it more effectively, it is imperative that the board members are familiar with the principles and recommended practices in the Sports Code.

Governance and funding are fundamentally linked. Good governance allows successful fundraising not only from the government and local authorities but also from the public and sponsors.

The Challenge of Compliance

In law, no training is required for a person to become a board member. In fact, a new board member of a company simply signs a form where they declare:

> 'I acknowledge that, as a board member, I have legal duties and obligations imposed by the Companies Act, other statutes and at common law.'[13]

And yet so often they have no idea what these legal duties and obligations are. The participants, the volunteers, the fans and the promoters, as well as the board members and the executive, need protection and they need protection from each other. They need to be trained in how a sporting entity should be governed.

Sport Ireland acknowledges that smaller NGBs may find the adoption of the Sports Code challenging. To assist, the Sport Ireland Organisational Development and Change Unit has undertaken a number of specific approaches to building the governance capability in the sports sector. These include:

- Advisory support
- Governance skills and knowledge training
- Step-by-step guides to implement the Sports Code, developed by the Carmichael Centre
- Annual conferences on governance

Implementing Change

Most board members aim to improve performance. However, there is the danger that governance just becomes a box-ticking exercise delegated to an individual or a committee and removed from the board. In order to implement change, it is vital that there is 'buy-in'. It is not good enough for the CEO to say that governance is very important and then delegate it to a junior member of staff or a committee to implement. They must understand it and ensure that it is understood by every member of the board. The entity will not benefit unless the whole board buys in.

If the process is derailed or half-heartedly supported by the board, the whole process becomes meaningless. Board members may see the introduction of new policies and systems as a threat and believe that such changes jeopardise their position. This, in fact, may be true if they were exercising unfettered power.

To get buy-in, it can help if the process is led by external people. Alternatively, existing skills on the board can be availed of, for instance a lawyer on the board might be asked to explain fiduciary duties.

Improving governance can be difficult as clubs and regions lack the resources to implement change and the status quo may seem acceptable. Ideally, the NGBs will encourage better governance in their affiliates and facilitate access to appropriate training.

Communication is vital to counter natural resistance to change. It would be naïve not to realise that in certain instances change is essential; for instance paying cash, using private PayPal accounts and not disclosing benefits in kind are not compatible with good governance.

The aim of the Sports Code is to raise standards. Good governance may be invisible to the members and fans but gradually the benefits of a well-run organisation should manifest themselves in better decision-making, transparency and accountability. Externally a well-run entity is seen as truly acting in the best interests of the sport and a proper custodian of the sport.

THE SMALLER ENTITY

Governance needs to be proportionate. The needs of a club, league, county or province differ from those of a large NGB. However governance is still important. Such entities may suffer from the unfettered power of an individual or group, lack of financial understanding, putting personal interests ahead of those of the club or poor appreciation of risk.

The Sports Code is divided into tiers or types. Type A is specifically designed for smaller entities and has less demanding governance requirements suitable for smaller sporting entities. A copy of the Type A Sports Code is included in the Appendix at the back of this book.

CONCLUSION

The need for good governance in all organisations is manifest. That is why the National Sports Policy 2018–2027 envisages that:

'Sport Ireland will oversee a process to have all National Governing Bodies and Local Sports Partnerships (LSPs) adopt the Governance Code for the Community, Voluntary and Charity Sector by end 2021. ... NGBs, LSPs and sports clubs can adopt the Code in accordance with their resources and capabilities to do so and in line with their strategic goals.'[14]

The next chapter looks at what enquiries to make before joining a board and the key roles in a sporting entity.

Ten Key Points

1. Sport Ireland is the statutory body established to plan and support the development of sport in Ireland. An NGB is the organisation 'recognised by its International Federation and/or World Federations for all aspects of the sport in Ireland'.

2. The Olympic Federation of Ireland's aim is to develop, promote and protect the Olympic movement in Ireland. The OFI has complete, independent control of all matters relating to the Olympics.

3. Governance simply means directing an entity. It is the system by which companies are directed and controlled.

4. Sporting entities need to be run according to best practice. The Sport Code aims to show what is best practice.

5. By 2021 the Sports Code will be mandatory for all entities funded by Sport Ireland. It is not mandatory for affiliated companies and non-funded bodies, although it is desirable that it is implemented at all levels of sport

6. The Sports Code concentrates on five principles:
    *   Leading the organisation
    *   Exercising control over the organisation
    *   Being transparent and accountable
    *   Working effectively
    *   Behaving with integrity

7. A board member must know if the sporting entity of which they are a board member is a company or if it is unincorporated.

8. If an entity is a company the board member has certain duties under the Companies Act.

9. Sporting entities may be governed badly because of the inexperience of the board members, failure to manage risk, lack of understanding and implementation of

financial controls, poor systems, lack of policies and poor reporting. Conflicts of interest remain a significant risk to good governance.

10. Governance is not a box-ticking exercise to be delegated to an individual or a committee and removed from the board. It sets out how a board should manage an entity.

PART II

BECOMING A BOARD MEMBER

2

BEFORE JOINING A BOARD

- Introduction
- Investigating the Organisation
- Board Members' Duties
- The Chair
- The Company Secretary
- Independent Board Members
- Types of Board Member
- Trustees
- The Smaller Entity
- Conclusion
- Ten Key Points

INTRODUCTION

This chapter looks at issues to consider before becoming a board member of a sporting organisation. Before joining a board, a potential board member should find out as much as possible about the entity and about the people they will be working with. This is called due diligence. It is simply the task of investigating an entity. The purpose of due diligence is so that potential board members understand the strengths and weaknesses of the entity they plan to join, and the risks involved. If possible, they should try to meet with key people in the entity, for instance the chair of the board and some or all of the other board members.

INVESTIGATING THE ORGANISATION

The idea of being a board member of a sporting organisation and influencing how a sport is run may seem attractive. However a potential board member should be careful. There are some serious questions to be asked before such a position is accepted. How much due diligence is necessary depends on the size and financial position of the entity.

A Potential Board Member Should Ask Themselves

Their Contribution

What will they bring to the board? The potential board member should be honest with themselves, asking why do they wish to become a board member or why have they been asked to become a board member. Are they only trying to become a board member to pursue their own personal sporting ambitions? Are they attracted by access to tickets, perks or the kudos of interacting with high-profile sportspeople? Did the person who invited them to go on the board simply want them to protect their position? Are they joining the board with the aim of disrupting the status quo? Do they really have something to contribute?

In sport, opinions can be fiercely divided, and this can be reflected on a board. While it is useful that there are a variety of opinions on a board, there can be strong characters and cliques. If a board member gets no personal satisfaction from being on a board or is unable to contribute, they may wonder why they are there. It may only be a matter of time before they cease to contribute to the success of the organisation, and perhaps become resentful or even distressed.

Time

Secondly, the potential board member must have the time to devote to the entity. Different entities take differing time commitments. A good estimate is to allow double what the organisation says it requires. If a board member has not had time to study the board information circulated prior to a meeting and has not completed their action points, then that board member is simply a drag on the organisation. The entity would be better off with a board member who has the time to address the issues. If a board member can find the time to turn up to a meeting, they should find the time to do their homework beforehand.

Many sporting entities are run on a volunteer basis. Being a volunteer does not give an excuse to not complete tasks in time. Importantly, the duties and responsibilities of a paid board member and a volunteer board member, in law, are identical.

Ask the Entity

Set out below is the information that should be sought from a sporting entity during due diligence.

Strategy[15]

An entity should have a written strategy, or at least a statement of its objectives and how it plans to achieve them. The strategy shows the potential board member the entity's plans for the next few years. Ideally the strategy should have clear performance measures included. A performance measure is a way of measuring the success of the board members in achieving the stated goals in the strategy.

Risk

On becoming a board member of a company, an individual potentially takes on personal liability. Personal liability is where the board member may themselves become liable for the debts or misdemeanours of the entity. One of the most important areas to check is solvency, i.e. has the entity enough money to continue in business and pay its debts as they fall due? If there are any concerns at all in this area it is essential to clarify the position and the risks before becoming a board member. If a sporting entity is in a fragile financial position, the board members may be personally liable if the company is found to be trading recklessly, i.e. trading when it knows it may not be able to pay its debts in time.

A related issue is to understand the key terms of any loans. Are these terms being met? Have government funds, including grants from Sport Ireland, been spent strictly in accordance with the terms? Most grants are given with a specific purpose and the potential board member needs to understand that grants can only be used for that purpose.

Not all risks are financial. A well-run entity should have a risk register detailing all the risks that face the entity. Other possible sporting risks might include safeguarding children, health and safety, doping, and disciplinary issues. If there is no risk register the potential board member should discuss risk with the chair or other board members to ensure that they understand the underlying risks.

Financial Reporting

All board members are responsible for the financials of an entity, not just the treasurer. The potential board member should always understand the finances before joining. If the potential board member has limited knowledge of financials, they should request the financials to be explained to them and ask the obvious questions – where does funding come from, how is it spent and how much money does the entity have at present?

The Structure[16]

All too often people leading sports organisations do not know what kind of entity it is. That's like playing a game and not knowing the rules. Is it a company? Or is it an unincorporated entity? The rules are different. An unincorporated entity means that it is not a company and therefore it is not subject to the Companies Act 2014. A company gives more protection to its members and board members in that their personal liability is limited. Generally, in an unincorporated entity the members are all personally liable and usually rely on insurance to mitigate risk. But in a company, liability for the members and the board members is limited, provided that they obey the law.

There are various different kinds of companies. The simplest – a limited company, with the abbreviation Ltd – can more or less do anything that an individual can do. A common form of company for a sporting entity is a company limited by guarantee or Clg. This means that the liability of its members is limited to the amount they have guaranteed, which is usually one euro per member. The powers of a Clg are set out in a written document, called the constitution; for instance it might state that it can or cannot borrow money.

It is also important to check whether the organisation is an NGB, a national governing body. As such it has duties outlined by Sport Ireland. The potential board member should check if Sport Ireland has carried out any audits of the entity or given any recommendations. They should also seek a copy of the most recent grant awards.

The Constitution[17]

Most entities, whether incorporated or unincorporated, have a constitution. An unincorporated entity may describe this document as 'rules', 'byelaws', or the 'founding document'. The constitution states what the entity can do and the basic rules of how the entity is to be run. It sets out the rules for members' meetings. It may give instructions about the running of board meetings and how board members are appointed and removed. Importantly, it may refer to reporting and control of finances. The constitution of a company may appear to be written in legalese. Some sporting entities have their sporting rules embedded in the constitution whereas others have a legal constitution and a separate set of sporting rules which deal with issues such as eligibility, competitions, disciplinary proceedings, high performance and committee structures. It is worth reading all these documents. A board member should not be acting if they do not know the rules.

It is often overlooked that a member of a company must be entered in the register of members. In a company it is very important to distinguish between a member of the company (within the meaning of the Companies Act) and members generally, i.e. the sporting members. They may be the same but not necessarily so. It is vital in company law to know who the members of the company are to invite to annual and extraordinary general meetings. The register must include the names and addresses of the members, the date on which each person was entered in the register as a member, and the date on which any person ceased to be a member.[18] The register must be kept up to date as failure to do so could be seized upon to challenge the validity of general meetings and voting at such meetings.

The constitution of a company limited by guarantee describes the objects of the entity. 'Objects' is just a legal word for the objectives. A potential board member should consider if they agree with these objectives and once they become a board member they should not do anything that is not included in the objectives. For instance, if the objects of a sporting entity are to promote their sport in Leinster, they should not develop that sport in Connaught.

The constitution sets out how elections of directors are run. The potential director should understand how the current directors have been elected. A potential board member must understand what powers they have and this depends on the type of entity they are on the board of.

Table 1: Legal Powers of Different Types of Entity

Type of Entity	Governed By	Power
Unincorporated entity	Rules/founding document/ constitution	Can do anything legal; personal liability is not limited
Limited company (Ltd)	Constitution/ Companies Act/ members' resolutions	Can do anything legal; personal liability is limited
Company Limited by Guarantee (Clg)	Constitution/ Companies Act/ members' resolutions	Board members should only act in accordance with the objectives set out in the constitution; personal liability is limited

Insurance

A common misconception is that insurance mitigates all risk. The claim process can be lengthy and 100 per cent of the risk may not be covered. Without question every entity should have appropriate public liability insurance and insurance for buildings and equipment where applicable. Most entities also have directors' and officers' insurance (D&O). D&O policies offer cover for board members and managers to protect them from claims which may arise from decisions taken within the scope of their regular duties. When assessing board membership, the potential board member should consider whether they consider the level of insurance adequate (see Chapter 7: Insurance).

Members have the best protection (see Chapter 7: Risks Associated with Not Incorporating) if the entity is a company, rather than an unincorporated entity, and has insurance.

Organisation's Staff/HR Structure

A potential board member should enquire into the staff structure. It is important that they understand their role and the parameters around the role. Are they to be executive? If so to what extent are they expected to act day-to-day? Are there terms of reference setting out the specific role of an executive board member? What interaction will they have with management? Or are they non-executive? How do they interface with the CEO? Useful documents to obtain in advance are the terms of reference of the board and the terms of reference of the chair and the CEO (see Chapter 9: The CEO – Roles and Responsibilities).

Clear reporting lines of management and committees are essential. It should be documented who reports to the board and when, and who can give instructions to an executive.

Summing Up the Investigation

It may not be possible to obtain all the information requested. As a very minimum it is essential to understand the solvency and major risks facing the entity. Just because an entity is a sporting entity does not mean that a potential board member should eschew due diligence. Ironically, the risks of joining a sporting board may be higher than that of a commercial company as financing may be tight and the board may be largely made up of people with sporting rather than corporate or financial expertise.

BOARD MEMBERS' DUTIES[19]

If the sporting entity is a company, then a board member, under company law, has certain specific duties. Yet does the board member know what their duties are? A board member who does not understand their duties should ensure that they get relevant training. Some companies run training for their board members, but smaller sporting organisations may expect a board member to come equipped with the knowledge.

The particular statute, or written law, that sets out many of the rules relating to how companies are run is the Companies Act 2014. There are eight fiduciary duties set out in the Act.[20] Fiduciary means that the board member is placed in a position of trust by the company, i.e. they are trusted to run the company and as such must exercise the highest standard of care.

These duties are set out in section 228 of the Companies Act and if a board member reads only one clause of the act it should be this one. The duties are:

- To act in good faith in what the board member considers to be the interests of the company
- To act honestly and responsibly in relation to the conduct of the affairs of the company
- To act in accordance with the company's constitution and exercise their powers only for the purposes allowed by law
- Not to use the company's property, information or opportunities for their own or anyone else's benefit
- Not to agree to restrict the board member's power to exercise independent judgement
- To avoid any conflict between the board member's duties to the company and their own interests
- To exercise the care, skill and diligence which would be exercised in the same circumstances by a reasonable person
- In addition to the duty to have regard to the interests of the company's employees in general, to have regard to the interests of its members

THE CHAIR[21]

The chair is responsible for leading the board and ensuring that it works effectively. They work to optimise the relationships between the board, the executive, volunteers and members. They need a good working knowledge of the constitution and the terms of reference of the officers and committees. A chair needs to be a good listener, a good role model and ideally a good public speaker. It is the chair who sets the ethical standards of the board and thus the whole entity. It is for the chair to motivate and listen to all members of the board.

On the other hand, the chair is constrained by their terms of reference. They must comply with the entity's policies and decisions. Being chair does not mean that they have a right to independent decision-making. The chair can only exercise those powers that have been delegated to the position by the board.

In some smaller organisations the chair also acts as the CEO, i.e. running the board and the executive. As an entity grows it is best practice for the board to step away from the day-to-day issues and concentrate on strategy, risk, monitoring and reporting. For instance, at Sport Ireland there is a board led by the chair, but there is also the executive team led by the CEO. In such sporting entities, the chair manages the board which gives instructions to the executive team. The chair should not trespass on the role of the CEO, who manages the executive team in accordance with the instructions from the board.

The chair should have a close and trusting relationship with the CEO, so they can challenge each other. It is preferable they collaborate strategically in the best interests of the organisation rather than attempting to be 'best friends' (see also Chapter 9: The CEO – Roles and Responsibilities).

The President

In some sporting entities there may be a chair running the board and there may also be a president who generally assumes a presidential/

ambassadorial role. However in other organisations the president also assumes the chair role, in which case the sporting entity needs to be careful that the president has the skills to act as chair.

THE COMPANY SECRETARY[22]

The company secretary is not a secretary in the normal meaning of the word. Under the Companies Act 2014 all companies, including sporting entities, must have a company secretary.[23] However, the Act sets out very limited duties for the company secretary and most duties are set by the board of directors.[24]

A non-board member, including a member of staff, but ideally not the CEO, may be considered for the company secretary role. Many small sporting entities, which are companies, use a professional firm to supply company secretarial tasks. The person appointed must be competent to fulfil the role and have the necessary skills, time and access to resources to carry out the role.[25] It is the responsibility of the board members to select an appropriate person.[26] The board members may ask the company secretary to take on additional duties such as supporting the board and its committees, preparing agendas and minutes, and organising general meetings. It should be noted that these are not statutory duties and can be delegated to another person, e.g. a secretary to the board.

As the role of the company secretary can be wider than set out in statute, written terms of reference are useful to define the role. These should be in place regardless of whether the company secretary is an external professional or a volunteer.

Because the company secretary is usually a person with professional experience or skills, they can be a useful contact person for the potential board member to discuss technical or legal issues with, particularly in smaller entities.

INDEPENDENT BOARD MEMBERS

Commercial bodies have availed of independent board members for many years. However, the idea of an independent board member is not yet standard practice in sporting entities. Board members on sporting boards often come from within the sport and few may have experience of running a company. Someone from outside may be resisted by the membership.

An independent board member helps monitor and control a company and makes sure it is running along the right lines, regardless of what sport it is involved in. They are useful whether or not the sport is incorporated. They improve decision-making by providing objective scrutiny and an external perspective. On the other hand, an independent board member needs good induction (see Chapter 3: Induction) and access to timely information so that they are able to make an objective assessment of any issue.

In a small sporting entity, the independent non-executive may 'do very little' but their help can be invaluable, for instance in:

- Ensuring that all company activities are addressed
- Selecting and working with auditors
- Smoothing a fallout between board members, or between the board members and the executive
- Facilitating the leaving of a board member or the recruiting of a new board member
- Offering encouragement when times are difficult
- Persuading the board to pay attention to cashflow management

The UK Code for Sports Governance demands at least 25 per cent of a board consists of independent non-executive board members.[27] This recognises that while it is important to have people on the board who understand the sport it is also important to have those who know how to run a company. In Ireland the two most recent reports into governance in the FAI and the Olympic Federation of Ireland both recommended the appointment of independent board members and while not mandatory at this stage the National Sports Policy makes specific reference to best governance practice including independent board members.[28]

TYPES OF BOARD MEMBER

Executive and Non-Executive Board Members

Different terms may be used to describe certain board members. The most important concept to understand is that of an executive board member compared to a non-executive board member. An executive board member is a person who is involved in the day-to-day running of the company, for instance the CEO, while a non-executive board member is not involved in the daily management.

Alternate Board Members

Alternate board members are sometimes used to represent a board member who cannot attend. While theoretically useful, there is the significant drawback that the alternate may not report back in full and may not have a good understanding of the leadership of the sport and the context of decisions being taken by the board. In addition, the person with whom they are alternating may not accept their judgement.

Representative or Nominee Board Members[29]

It can often be challenging when the new board member has been nominated by a special interest group, e.g. by a region or province, by a big donor of the sport or in certain sports, e.g. horse racing and horse sports, by the government. A feature of sporting boards is that a majority of board members are likely to be representative. Such a board member may be described as a nominee or representative. A potential nominee board member of a sporting entity should consider any possible conflicts of interest in advance and discuss with the nominating party and the entity.

Nominees, just as other board members, are expected to act in the interest of the entity. A board member may be nominated by a particular group or person, but they must not act as a representative of that group when acting as a board member. Instead, they should promote the aims of the sporting entity in line with its constitution or rules. Furthermore, as a board member they must at all times respect board confidentiality. This can generate a conflict of interest with the entity that they represent. There is, however, nothing to stop a director of one entity, affiliated or not, from being a director of another entity. If a conflict of interest does arise it should be treated in line with the conflict of interests policy of the relevant entity.

De Facto Board Members

When considering joining a board, the potential board member needs to consider the concept of a 'de facto board member'. A person may wish to be involved in decision-making at board meetings but not be a board member or member. For instance, a lawyer or accountant may be worried about poor governance in an organisation and not want to be a formal board member as it might reflect on their professional persona. Similarly, a well-known athlete or individual in a sport, for instance a coach or a commentator, might not wish to lend their name until the organisation is established. However, by being involved in decision-making they are in effect a de facto board member. De facto board members are defined in law as 'a person who occupies the position of director of a company but who has not been formally appointed as such director'.[30] This person is not in fact escaping their liability and obligations as a board member in law. They are equally responsible for the decisions of the board.

TRUSTEES

An entity that is not a company but a collection of individuals often appoints trustees to hold property. The constitution should set out the rules for the appointment of trustees – how many and whether they are appointed for life or a fixed term. Equally important is the removal of trustees. If they are appointed for life, there must be terms allowing for their replacement should they become inactive or non-compliant.

Trustees only have the powers that are delegated to them by the sporting entity. They cannot act beyond those powers. An indemnity is usually given to the trustee by the entity but the indemnity is usually limited to the role of trustee so if the trustee goes beyond the scope of their role then the indemnity may be denied. They typically may have the powers to acquire and dispose of land, to lease, to borrow and to insure.

Title deeds are registered in the individual trustee's name, but the deed giving them title should clearly indicate that the property is in trust for the benefit of the club.

If the entity is sued, usually the trustees are named as they hold the property. Trustees should be aware that if the assets of the club are insufficient to discharge the liability that they may be personally liable. To protect the trustee there should be members' indemnity and appropriate insurance.

THE SMALLER ENTITY

Due Diligence

Some due diligence should be done even before joining a small club. It is essential to check the financial position of the club and if there are any outstanding complaints or grievances, or even legal cases.

The potential board member must understand what kind of entity it is,[31] i.e. is it a company – if so what kind of company; is it a provident society; or is it just a committee? They should get a copy of the constitution.[32]

They should check that there is public liability insurance or buildings insurance and whether there is a D&O policy.[33]

The Chair

The chair is particularly important in a smaller entity where members may be less used to the formal environment of board meetings. The chair keeps order at meetings, encourages participation and ensures that decisions are made.[34] The potential board member should meet with the chair and discuss the entity before joining.

Nominee Board Members

Board members must understand that while they were nominated by a particular group, they must not act as a representative of that group when acting as a board member. Instead, they should promote the aims of the organisation in line with its governing document.[35] This does not prevent them, when relevant or requested, from expressing the views of their representative group.

Trustees

Trustees are commonly used in clubs to own property. The potential board member should understand their role and the deed appointing them.

CONCLUSION

Whether to become a board member is an important decision and one that should not be entered into blindly. The potential board member should make detailed enquiries into how the entity is run and understand the risks involved and the duties of a director. The next chapter considers first steps once the decision is made to join.

Ten Key Points

1. When considering joining a board a potential board member should reflect on what they can contribute to the board and if they really have the time to contribute.

2. Due diligence is essential but should be proportionate to the size and role of the entity.

3. No matter what size the sporting entity is, the potential board member should understand its financial position and solvency.

4. Members have the best protection if the entity is a company, rather than an unincorporated entity, and has insurance.

5. If the sporting entity is a company, a board member has specific fiduciary duties set out in the Companies Act 2014. Fiduciary means that they are operating in a position of trust rather than for themselves, i.e. they are operating on behalf of the company, not themselves.

6. The chair is responsible for leading the board and ensuring that it works effectively.

7. The company secretary is not a secretary in the normal meaning of the word but has certain statutory duties. A company secretary should have the appropriate skills to carry out their role.

8. An independent board member helps monitor and control an entity and makes sure it is running along the right lines, regardless of what sport it is involved in. The board member, ideally, should come from outside the sport.

9. A de facto board member is 'a person who occupies the position of director of a company but who has not been formally appointed as such director'. It does not matter that they have not been formally identified as a board member. In law, they are equally responsible for the decisions of the company.

10. An entity that is not a company but a collection of individuals often appoints trustees to hold property.

3

ON JOINING THE BOARD

- Introduction
- Induction
- Matters Reserved for the Board
- The Board as Leader
- Committees
- The Smaller Entity
- Conclusion
- Ten Key Points

INTRODUCTION

This chapter looks at issues to be considered on joining the board of a sporting entity. Ideally the new board member investigated the organisation, spoke to members of the board and executive and reviewed any public information about the entity before joining. They may have been given access to some internal information but, until the board member joins, it will not have been possible to obtain all the information desired. Having joined the board, the board member should now try to get up to speed as fast as possible.

Induction describes the process of the entity allocating time specifically to teach new board members about the company. Even if the entity is small and there is no formal induction process, a new board member should specifically ask for a meeting to learn about key issues.

This chapter also considers the policies and committees that a board member would expect to find in a reasonable-sized sporting entity. The number of such policies and committees depends on the size and structure of the entity.

INDUCTION[36]

The purpose of the induction process is to ensure that the new board members understand the entity, the sport and their role as a board member. This enables them to become an effective member of the board as soon as possible. Ideally induction is tailored to fit the knowledge and experience of the board member. For instance, a board member from a sports background may need time to understand the constitution and the financial statements, while a board member with an accounting background may need more information about the sport itself.

Induction should cover:

- The sport
- The organisation's structure and history
- The Sports Code
- Strategy
- The role of the board
- The financial position and source of funds
- Risk
- Policies

- The constitution
- Matters reserved for board decisions

It is useful if the entity prepares an induction pack with the above information. It may be worth considering initially pairing a new board member with an existing board member who has the opposite skills, e.g. a new board member who is an accountant with a board member from the sporting side.

Letter of Appointment[37] and Registers

On appointment the board member should be given a letter of appointment, confirming their role, the policies and particularly the ethics of the entity and the time that they are expected to commit to the organisation. If the entity is a company the letter should also remind the newly appointed board member of their fiduciary duties (see Chapter 2: Board Members' Duties). Fiduciary duties are 'the legal duties of one party to act in the best interests of another', i.e. for the board member to act in the interests of the company. The board member will be asked to sign a B10 form for the Companies Registration Office and provide information relating to any other board memberships they may already have. Board members are normally also asked to sign a code of conduct and a conflicts of interest declaration.

It is important to ensure in a company that the new board director's details are entered in the company's own register of directors. If the new director also becomes a member, the register of members must also be updated. Failure to register a director, although an offence, does not invalidate the director's status as a director. However it should be noted that the CRO does not keep a company's registers. It is the responsibility of the company to maintain its registers.

If the new director is also a 'managing official' as set out by the money laundering legislation then the person must also be added to the Register of Beneficial Owners (see Chapter 9: Financial Obligations).

The Sport

Historically most board members on a sporting board have come from within the sport. Increasingly, good governance is encouraging the involvement of some board members from outside the sport who may have a fresh independent view and some specific skills useful in running an entity effectively, e.g. marketing, finance, law and governance. Induction should explain the sport and how it is structured. This may also be useful for board members who have been involved in the sport at a low level and know little about the complexities of national and international competition. Similarly, board members who come from the international side of the sport may have moved away from the day-to-day problems facing the sport in clubs locally.

The Organisation's Structure and History

The new board member needs to understand the legal structure of the entity and how the entity evolved. Familiarity with the history of the entity may help to understand legacy issues, e.g. why there are a very high number of members of the board. Induction should cover all the major stakeholders, e.g. the government, donors, elite athletes, fans and volunteers.

Sports Code[38]

The Governance Code (aka the Sports Code) is there to help board members govern, i.e. run their entity.

'Corporate governance provides the structure through which the objectives of the company are set and the means of attaining those objectives and monitoring performance are determined.'[39]

The induction process should familiarise the new board member with the Sports Code and explain how far the entity is in achieving compliance with the Sports Code.

Strategy[40]

Ideally the induction pack includes the strategy and a recent assessment of the completion of strategic objectives. Smaller clubs may not have a written strategy. Their year may be determined by a couple of large events. However even the smallest club should have a work plan with targets, timelines, the budget and details of proposed funding and plans as to how they can grow. These should reflect the objectives set out in the founding document or in the constitution.

The Role of the Board and Individual Board Members[41]

The role of the board is to lead the entity and to concentrate on strategy, risk, monitoring and accountability. Individual board members may have specific skills, e.g. a finance board member or a PR board member. A brief biography of the board and top management and an organisation chart is useful on induction. Ideally this information would be on the organisation's website.

Terms of Reference[42]

There should be written terms of reference for the board and also for individual board members. In the terms of reference for the CEO the division of responsibility between the board and the executive must be clear. The terms of reference simply outlines what that person or group is responsible for.

A small sports organisation should document the role of the chair, the secretary and the treasurer at least.

The Separation of the Executive and Non-Executive[43]

In larger entities the executive (i.e. those who handle day-to-day matters) should be separate with the board monitoring its performance, i.e. the board is non-executive. Often the board is volunteer but the executive is paid. Mid-sized sporting entities may have one or two paid executives, perhaps a CEO or managing board member, secretary or treasurer, with the remainder of the executive being volunteers.

A club may have volunteer hands-on board members with no clear CEO. There is no particular moment in time when the board should be separated from the executive, but it does help even in smaller entities to separate the running of competitions from the running of the entity.

The new board member, where the executive is separate, should not interfere with executive duties that are properly delegated to staff. The chair and CEO should have terms of reference and each member of staff should have a job description showing their executive duties and to whom they report. On the other hand, the executive is always accountable to the board through the CEO (see Chapter 9: The CEO – Roles and Responsibilities).

As the entity grows, board members become responsible for overview of and monitoring the executive. The idea of a monitoring board can be fiercely resisted by the executive. They may argue that this is not a traditional structure for sport, that it is a commercial structure, a business structure. However, as the emphasis grows on financial control and good governance the role of the board in leading and monitoring becomes increasingly important.

Financial Position and Funding[44]

Solvency

During induction the new board member must concentrate on the main risks that are facing the company. Most important is solvency. Is what they understood during their due diligence correct? If there are solvency risks – and unfortunately, as sports are often constrained for funds, this is common – the board member must understand the financing and cashflow of the entity.

They may have been told that the bank is 'on side', but now they are in the company they should inspect any documents or agreements with the bank or even ask to meet the bank. Similarly, the entity may be relying on a particular sponsor. But what evidence is there that the sponsor is still supportive?

Financial Statements and Controls

The induction of the new board member should include a copy of the accounts and a thorough review of the finances, particularly if the new board member does not have a financial background. The new board member should also be aware of the financial controls within the organisation – who is authorised to make payments, signatories and control levels. All board members are equally responsible for the finances, not just the financial board member or treasurer. Therefore, if the new board member does not understand the figures they should ask for help from a fellow board member, treasurer or auditor to interpret them.

Tax Status

Most sporting entities are granted a Sports Body Tax Exemption by the Revenue. The member should understand the implications of this, in particular in relation to the payment of directors (see Chapter 9: Tax).

Risk[45]

The new board member may have become aware of risks during the due diligence process and at that point accepted assurances. Now having joined the entity they must double-check those assurances. Ideally the entity has a risk register and the new board member can be talked through the risks facing the entity. They should enquire into any legal, employee or ethical issues which perhaps the entity was reluctant to discuss in the interests of confidentiality until the board member was on the board.

The new board member should be particularly sensitive at this time that they are being told the whole truth. It may be that the existing board members may not wish to burden the new board member too early or the existing board members may believe, erroneously, that an issue is confidential and should be disclosed on a need-to-know basis. On the other hand, a new board member needs to make an assessment quickly whether they are happy to remain a board member of the entity, as in law all board members are equally liable.

Board Policies[46]

Every entity should have a range of policies laying out internal procedures. Ideally these should be published on the website; as a minimum there should be a constitution, a statement on equality, the code of conduct including confidentiality, and a health and safety statement. The terms of reference of any committee should also be published and those of the key roles – the chair, the treasurer and the secretary.

There can be a lot of resistance to having such policies and terms of reference available transparently. It is true that, sadly, there can be members or stakeholders who enjoy the sport of debating/disputing policies rather than furthering the success of the sport. However, in a transparent and accountable sporting entity the underlying policies should be available to all members and stakeholders. The board should not guard such terms of reference as confidential or as an internal matter.

Smaller sporting entities should keep their policies simple. It can become an expensive and time-wasting activity if lawyers, mediators or arbitrators are necessary to interpret the club's own rules. However there should be policies to comply with all legal requirements, e.g. health and safety.

During induction, policies should be explained to the new board members and they may be asked to sign a document stating that they have read and understood them.

Policy on Conflicts of Interest or Loyalty[47]

A conflict of interest is where board members' other professional or private interests might clash with their duty to the company, e.g. the member's family may sell containers and the club is at present considering buying a container to house their equipment.

An example of a conflict of loyalty would be where the board member represents a sponsor and therefore their decisions may be or may be perceived to be influenced by loyalty to the sponsor rather than to the interests of the company. For instance, if the sponsor is considering withdrawing their support unless the company takes a certain action that is not in the entity's strategic plan.

Similarly, a conflict can occur when the interests of those who elected the new director to the board may be given precedence over the interests of the sport.

A policy on conflicts of interest or loyalty sets out the steps that a board member should take if they are aware of a conflict of interest or loyalty.

Policy on Confidentiality[48]

Board members must maintain the confidentiality of any personal or sensitive information that they acquire while acting as a board member. It is the board members' duty to act honestly at all times and in the interests of the company and therefore not to disclose confidential information. A policy defines what is confidential information and the procedures for dealing with stakeholders or the media (see Chapter 8: Board Confidentiality).

Data Protection Policy[49]

With the advent of GDPR (the EU's General Data Protection Regulation, which became law in May 2018) an entity must have clear rules as to how it complies with the law. During induction new board members should be made aware of sensitive areas relating to data protection, e.g. photographing children, not sending out emails which show all recipients' email addresses. This is a useful area for all board members to get training on.

Financial Policy

The financial policy sets out who can sign cheques, use online banking, what limits are in place for authorisation and who can use a credit card, if anyone. It should also cover financial reporting deadlines. A larger organisation may have monthly or quarterly financial reviews and comparisons to budget.

Employment Policy[50]

This policy sets out an organisation's guidelines on the employment of individuals. The guidelines on 'recruitment, induction, supervision and appraisals and the grievance and disciplinary procedures may be in one or more documents.'[51]

There should be formal arrangements for the ongoing supervision and development of staff with appraisals carried out at least annually.

Equality Policy[52]

This policy ensures that there is no discrimination against any individual or group (see Chapter 9: People Issues). Bullying, harassment and gender diversity policies may be included in this policy or be separate policies in themselves. An example of the need for such a policy is the November 2018 investigation into a French soccer club over the alleged racial profiling of players by its scouts.[53]

Health and Safety Policy[54]

This policy sets out safety procedures, risk assessments and what to do in case of an accident. There may be additional protocols relating to concussion, animal welfare, or maintenance of vehicles as may be relevant to the individual sport. An individual should be identified as responsible for health and safety on the board. A small club should consider health and safety aspects of activities and put a plan in place to deal with any problems. At the very minimum fire, ambulance and nearest hospital details should be available at all times.

Volunteer Policy[55]

'A policy dealing with the recruitment, induction, support and supervision of volunteers and setting out the procedures for implementing the policy and dealing with problems, if they arise.'[56]

Whistleblowing Policy[57]

This allows staff to raise concerns in confidence about possible improprieties about matters of public interest where that knowledge is gained through their employment.

Code of Conduct[58]

This policy sets out the expected standard of behaviour of members and board members and the procedures if these are not adhered to. A code of ethics may be incorporated into this document or an additional document. A code of ethics encourages the discussion and handling of ethical dilemmas that the board member or members may encounter. The code should cover the receipt of and the giving of gifts as well as hospitality.

Disciplinary Policy

This policy, unlike employment disciplinary procedures (which relate to employees), sets out how breaches of rules by members or breaches of sporting rules are handled by the organisation. The policy should also set out how appeals will be handled for such cases and who will manage and hear the case on behalf of the organisation.

Other Policies

The above is not a comprehensive list of internal policies. Depending on the sport there may be other appropriate ones, e.g. social media, travel, bribery, money laundering, food preparation, coaching.

MATTERS RESERVED FOR THE BOARD[59]

Matters reserved for the board are the decisions that only the board can make, and which cannot be delegated to an individual or committee. They are generally set out in a specific policy document. They relate to issues that are so important or significant to the sporting entity that the day-to-day management or the chair should not take the decision in isolation but only with the agreement of the board.

The executive team – i.e. the people working day-to-day or the volunteers on the ground – needs to have some discretion, but the limits of its authority should be defined. For example, in a local hockey club the day-to-day team may be responsible for buying new hockey balls but would not have the authority to decide upon a major renovation to the club house, which would be a matter reserved for the board.

A typical list of matters reserved for the board may include:

- Approval of the granting or acceptance of loans
- Approval of strategy and monitoring delivery thereof

- The annual budget and business plan
- Approving the financial statements
- Long-term investments
- Large capital projects
- Engagement with stakeholders
- Appointment and removal of board members or key personnel
- Terms of reference of any committees
- Approval of new policies
- Financial authority of individuals or committees
- Board members' training
- Approval of the list of matters reserved for the board

Board members should be aware that some financial restrictions, such as a specific person only making bank transfers of up to a certain limit, are not always effective, as it is easy to make transfers on successive days. When deciding limits and financial policies such practices need to be considered by the board.

All policies, roles and terms of reference of committees should be reviewed at least bi-annually. While this might sound too frequent for a small entity, it does not mean a rewrite; it just means that everyone re-reads the policy and checks that it is still relevant. This review should include membership of committees and the skills of the board. Committee members can be changed by a decision of the board (if provided for in the constitution) but weaknesses on the board should be referred to the nomination committee, if there is one.

Accountability

Matters reserved for the board are important as the board members of an entity are ultimately accountable for the entity. The board members can delegate tasks to specific specialised committees, the CEO or the executive, but they cannot delegate accountability.

THE BOARD AS LEADER

It is the board that drives the decisions in a sporting organisation. It, not the CEO and the executive, is the ultimate decision-making body. It is responsible for monitoring while the executive is responsible for operations. The board is also responsible for ensuring that the CEO or other key members of the executive, e.g. a high-performance manager, remain within the authority that is granted to them and that no board member or member of the executive wields unrestricted power.

The board members must at all times act in the best interests of the sport. The chair should ensure that the voice of each board member is heard and that no one board member monopolises a discussion.

Collective Responsibility[60]

The board members of an entity are collectively responsible for the running of the entity. This means that every board member is responsible for decisions of the board, even if they individually have disagreed with a decision and voted against it in the boardroom.

Collective responsibility can be a difficult concept. Board members may struggle to understand that in the boardroom they must act in the interests of the sport and not their individual region or club. They may wrongly wish it to be known publicly that they disagreed with a decision. The growth and success of a sport depends on all board members acting for the good of the sport. Individuals need to support decisions made as a group rather than insisting on their personal views and they need to take responsibility and ownership of decisions that they may personally disagree with.

Leadership

The role of the board is to lead the entity. The board sets the strategic objectives of the company and ensures that there are resources to achieve these objectives. The board is there to ensure that all risks to the entity are considered and that there are effective controls. The board monitors the performance of the entity and reports to the members or shareholders of the entity. In short, the role of the board and each board member on the board is to address:

- Strategy
- Risk
- Monitoring
- Accountability

A board member runs a sporting entity on behalf of the members. Their priority is the entity itself. If the entity is a company the names of new board members need to be submitted to the CRO (Companies Registration Office) and this information is public knowledge. Board members' names appear on all letters and in the accounts.

A board member is expected to attend all board meetings. The annual report should show how many meetings the board member has attended. If attendance is poor the chair should discuss with them why they are not engaged, or the members remove them when their turn for re-election comes up.

COMMITTEES

There should be formal terms of reference for all committees agreed by the board. For transparency these terms of reference should be on the organisation's website and reports on their work made available. The board delegates tasks to a committee but cannot delegate responsibility, i.e. any decision that the committee takes needs to be approved by the board or within delegated authority.

Committees should be formed as the board considers necessary to support its work. In sporting entities committees may be formed to give expert advice on specialist sport-specific issues, e.g. high performance, referees, judging, safeguarding children. A committee may have members who are experts and bring specialist skills. They need not be members of the board. Membership of a committee is also ideal training for future board members and leaders in the sport.

Below is a list of common committees in larger sporting entities. In many entities some of these committees may be combined, e.g. board review and governance. It is useful for board members to be involved in specific areas of expertise and play an active role on committees. On the other hand, the board may invite experts, whether internal or external, onto committees. In a smaller entity, a committee may be the whole board or a couple of designated people to look at a particular issue.

Audit Committee[61]

The audit committee is a board committee in that it is a committee that reports direct to the board. Its role is to monitor and if necessary make appropriate recommendations to the board on:

- The accuracy of the financial statements of the organisation
- Announcements about the organisation's financial performance and financial controls
- Control and risk management systems
- The effectiveness of the organisation's internal audit role
- The external auditor's independence and the effectiveness of the audit process.
- Arrangements for staff to raise concerns in confidence about possible improprieties relating to financial reporting

This is a useful committee to have independent experts on. It should never be combined with the finance committee as it acts as a check on the finance committee. Even in a small sporting entity it is useful for a second person, who is not the treasurer or finance board member but who has some financial knowledge, to review the financial statements and follow up any external auditor comments on controls. This person does not necessarily need to be a board member. (For more on audit committees see Chapter 7: Role of the Internal Auditor and Audit Committee.)

Finance Committee[62]

This is a common sub-committee in sporting organisations where there may be low level of financial knowledge on the board. It must be emphasised that this committee should not replace the board and that its terms of reference, and in particular its level of financial authority, must be clearly defined. The chair of the committee should ensure that all decisions are adequately explained to the board and cannot be actioned without board approval unless they are within the delegated authority to the committee from the board. The board, even when delegating tasks, remains responsible for all decisions. While it can be intimidating to question the recommendations of a specialist group, a board member should never hesitate to ask a financial question as each board member carries financial responsibility.

The finance committee must ensure that there are appropriate financial and management controls. Controls can be as simple as having different levels of authority or that certain duties are always separate – e.g. that someone senior, as well as the person doing the accounting, has access to the bank statements.

The committee considers the income and expenditure of the entity, setting budgets and investigating differences or unexpected movements, and reports thereon to the board. The committee reviews the effectiveness of investments before recommending them to the board, e.g. is it worth renting or investing in a new playing field.

The finance committee must ensure compliance with the terms and conditions of any public or private grants or donations received.

The finance committee is responsible for the preparation of the accounts. However, the accounts are signed by two board members on behalf of all members of the board.

This can be a powerful committee and the board should always ensure that it acts within its remit and that the board is updated on a timely basis.

Risk Committee

The risk committee is a board committee and is responsible for risk management. This includes assessing key areas of risk; reviewing, reporting on and managing risk; recommending to the board appropriate levels and appetite of risk; consideration of mitigation of risks, e.g. through insurance; and investigating failures in internal controls. A risk register should be prepared and updated at least quarterly. Insurance companies may seek sight of this register before underwriting risk.

The risk committee is sometimes combined with the audit committee or the governance committee.

Governance Committee

A governance committee is involved in providing support to the board in ensuring that the organisation is compliant across a number of areas – e.g. company law, employment law, safeguarding children, data protection, governance audit reviews and many more. The governance committee is there to implement and then to review adherence to the Sports Code. The committee should report on its work to the board and highlight any areas of concern or non-compliance. If the Sports Code has been adopted the workings of the board and the executive should be assessed at least annually to ensure that the entity is still compliant with recommended practice.

Rules Committee

The rules of an organisation should be reviewed annually. This involves a review of legislation, consideration of the overall structure of the organisation, and consideration of recommendations from Sport Ireland and also from coaches, referees, judges and members.

This exercise can involve considerable consultation and therefore a clear process should be set out in the terms of reference of the committee.

Board Review Committee[63]

There should be a specific committee responsible for the running of the board and in particular reviewing its terms of reference and matters reserved for the board as well as evaluation of board performance. This committee should take responsibility for induction, training and board evaluations.

Remuneration Committee

If the entity wishes to avail of an exemption from corporation tax remuneration cannot be paid to board members of a sporting organisation. There should be a remuneration committee to deal with salaries of senior management. The decision on salaries, including pensions and bonuses, should be a matter reserved for the board, although the board may issue general guidance on salary levels/budget availability and authorise the HR committee/ CEO to approve certain salaries within levels and report back to the board.

This committee is often combined with the HR committee.

Human Resources (HR) Committee

An HR committee is responsible for HR policies, e.g. on recruitment, pay and conditions of employment, staff relations including disciplinary and grievance procedures, staff development and equality. There should also be clear policies on social media, email usage, data protection, CCTV and whistleblowing.

Nomination Committee

This is a board committee which identifies and makes recommendations to the board on candidates for senior positions in the company. It considers the composition of the board and succession plans with the aim of improving or maintaining the board members' effectiveness. As board members are elected by the members it is responsible for presenting recommendations to the members.

When assessing board appointments, the nomination committee should evaluate the skills currently available to the board and the capabilities and experience required. This is one committee where the presence of independent non-executive board members gives assurance to stakeholders, ensuring that the process is objective. The size of the nomination committee is up to the board, but it is commonly made up of three people. In a smaller entity the nomination committee may consist of the whole board, ideally including an independent board member.

Specialist Sporting Committees

Sporting entities may also have specialist committees, such as:

- Technical
- Medical
- Athletes/player
- Judges/referees
- Coaching
- Safeguarding children
- High performance
- Building/infrastructure maintenance

THE SMALLER ENTITY

Induction

Induction[64] at a small sporting entity may simply mean meeting the chair, who explains the work of the board and its committees and helps the new board member to get involved. The new board member should ensure that they get a copy of the constitution and the rules. If the constitution is written in 'legalese' they should ask for help reading it. They should familiarise themselves with the Sports Code for Type A entities.

They should ensure that they understand the key risks and how they are managed[65] as well as any data protection issues and most importantly safeguarding children.[66]

Policies and Committees

A smaller entity would be expected to have 'policies', which may be simply one page, on conflicts of interest,[67] confidentiality,[68] data protection,[69] equality,[70] health and safety,[71] volunteers[72] and a code of conduct.[73]

There may be small groups of board members and volunteers who work on a particular issue, e.g. rules, governance, building maintenance. While an audit committee would be excessive, it is useful to have a person with financial knowledge, who is not the treasurer or finance board member, to review the accounts and follow up any external auditor comments on controls. This person does not necessarily need to be a board member.

Equality is just as important in a smaller entity and the board should actively consider the participation of women in the club, its ability to cater for disabled members and not discriminate. Even in a small club the board members should make sure activities are as accessible as possible.

The smaller entity should decide and record how decisions are taken at meetings and between meetings.[74]

CONCLUSION

As soon as a board member takes up their role it is important to understand the entity and how it works. This includes understanding what matters are reserved for the board and what is the role of the executive as opposed to the board. A new board member should take time to read and understand all board policies.

The next chapter looks at how meetings of the board should be run.

Ten Key Points

1. The purpose of the induction process is to ensure that the new board members understand the entity, the sport and their role as a board member.

2. The role of the board is to lead the entity and to concentrate on strategy, risk, monitoring and accountability.

3. On appointment the board member should be given a letter of appointment outlining their role, and the time that they are expected to commit to the organisation. They should confirm their understanding of the policies and particularly the ethics of the entity.

4. The induction of a new board member should include a copy of the accounts and a thorough review of the finances, particularly if the new board member does not have a financial background. All board members are equally responsible for the finances, not just the financial board member or treasurer.

5. The Sports Code is there to help leaders govern, i.e. run their entity. It is there to guide the board members.

6. Every entity should have a range of policies laying out internal procedures, i.e. how things are done in the organisation.

7. Matters reserved for the board are the decisions that only the board can make and which cannot be delegated to an individual or committee.

8. The board members of an entity form the board and they are collectively responsible for the running of the entity. This means that every board member is responsible for decisions of the board, even if they individually

have disagreed with a decision and voted against it in the boardroom.

9. The board members can delegate tasks but not accountability to committees. Committees allow a particular focus on areas that need specialist attention and time. All committees should have clear terms of reference describing their role, membership and responsibilities.

10. The finance committee is a common sub-committee in sporting organisations. It must be emphasised that this committee should not replace the board and that its terms of reference and in particular its level of financial authority must be clearly defined in the terms of reference. It should not be amalgamated with the audit committee.

4

FIRST MEETING AS A BOARD MEMBER

- Introduction
- How Meetings Should Be Run
- The Role of the Chair in Meetings
- Updates on Activities
- After the Meeting
- Culture
- The Smaller Entity
- Conclusion
- Ten Key Points

INTRODUCTION

The new board member has investigated the sporting entity, signed up as a board member and attended induction. It is now time for their first board meeting.

It is the role of the chair to set the agenda, control the meeting and ensure that it ends on time.

There is nothing worse than a poorly run meeting with the agenda handed out at the meeting, a paper read aloud, a couple of people monopolising the floor and the meeting going on for an hour or two longer than scheduled. The key to a well-run board meeting is a strong chair and a well-planned agenda. The chair needs to be ruthless in insisting that papers are produced before the meeting, and that they have been read beforehand so the time of the meeting can be used for analysis. Action points need to be not only recorded but also followed up on.

Board members should not tolerate poor board meetings and should put pressure on the chair to take control.

HOW MEETINGS SHOULD BE RUN

Dates[75]

The first task is to decide the dates in advance. It is a waste of time everyone trying to coordinate diaries at a board meeting. The board should meet sufficiently regularly to ensure that the entity is run effectively. This would normally be every six weeks to two months. The number of meetings may be included in the terms of reference of the board or outlined in its constitution.

The constitution or terms of reference of the board may stipulate instructions for running board meetings. Board members can change the terms of reference of the board by a board decision, but any directions in the constitution can only be changed by a meeting of members and if the entity is a company it would require a 75 per cent majority vote.

At the beginning of the year it is helpful if a board meeting calendar is drawn up ensuring that key issues are to be addressed at certain meetings during the year. This ensures that dates are secured in board members' diaries and that all areas are covered.

Agenda[76]

The agenda is prepared by the chair in consultation with the board secretary and the executive, usually represented by the CEO. The board secretary may be the company secretary but does not have to be. The board secretary has the specific role of serving the board.

When preparing the agenda, the secretary should take careful consideration of actions outstanding. An action is a decision taken at a board meeting that a task needs to be completed. The task is allocated to a specific individual responsible for completing the task by a certain date. Before the meeting the secretary should get an update from all members as to what actions have been addressed since the last meeting. Tasks should not be cleared from the action list until the board agrees that the task is complete or has changed.

Requests for items to be included on the agenda from other board members or the management may be considered but it is ultimately a decision of the chair as to what is included. An agenda might include:

- The minutes of the last meeting
- Outstanding action points that have not been completed from previous meetings
- Strategic issues
- Finances and funding
- Governance
- Membership issues
- Stakeholder issues
- Health and safety issues
- Disciplinary issues
- Facilities management
- Sport report

- Reports from committees
- Investments/special projects
- Risks
- Sponsorship
- Communications and media
- Athlete, sponsor and NGB issues

Strategic Issues[77]

The board should monitor performance against the strategic plan. (For more on the strategic plan please see Chapter 6: Strategy.)

Finances

The financial position should be addressed at every meeting. In this way those who are not comfortable with figures become familiar with the finances. A small club's finances are largely income and expenditure accounts and board members should be told what has been received or paid. In larger clubs reporting should be done by certain key performance indicators (see Chapter 6: Measuring Success and Key Performance Indicators).

Governance

This may include updating the board on the Sports Code and proposing new policies for the board to examine. It may also include a regular review of policy documents and consideration of areas which the board may wish to seek independent advice on.

Membership

Membership issues may include how to attract more members or how to keep members. It may include an analysis of underage participation and the resources and training required. Many sports organisations are subscription-based and the collection of subscriptions can be a time-consuming exercise. The board may need to consider how to make this as straightforward as possible.

Stakeholders

Issues may include liaison with donors, reporting on adherence to grant conditions, PR and local community initiatives. Sporting entities, by their nature, are particularly dependent on grants and donors and therefore close relationships with stakeholders are essential. Donors might be invited to the Christmas dinner or to one of the entity's main events. It is essential that the entity shows its appreciation.

Disciplinary Issues[78]

The board should ensure that there is a clear system for handling complaints, both employee and member complaints and external complaints. Employee complaints should be dealt with separately under an employee handbook and employee policies in line with good HR practice and legislation.

Complaints relating to members and the sport itself should be dealt with via a specific disciplinary policy. It helps if the complaint is dealt with swiftly by a senior person in the organisation.

While each entity should ensure that it has adequate disciplinary, complaints and appeals procedures in place, these rules can quickly be challenged and lawyers become involved in interpretation of the sporting entity's rules. In a fractious dispute an entity can spend a lot of money on the interpretation of its own rules. It does help to remove the issue from the immediate management or the board to external arbitration or mediation.

All complaints should be logged. The log should each year be reviewed to ensure that the system for dealing with complaints is working.

Safeguarding children issues must be directly reported to Tusla if there are any concerns (see Chapter 9: Safeguarding Children and Young People). If weaknesses in policies and operations are subsequently found, then it becomes a matter for the board to address.

Unfortunately, many sporting entities suffer from disputes. This is an extremely stressful area and can take up an inordinate amount of board and executive time. Disputes may be as simple as a member breaking the rules but very quickly that person's supporters may become active on social media. The issue can rapidly divide an entity, causing huge PR damage and expense. It can become particularly difficult when a board member, elected by the members, is one of the disputing parties.

If the complainant wants to take the issue further there should be a clear path for escalation quickly leading to Sport Dispute Solutions Ireland. Sport Ireland requires that NGBs must include a clause for disciplinary appeals to be directed to SDSI.[79] The key is to move quickly and according to agreed procedure and to consider all options. Even though it may initially appear expensive it may be worth quickly referring a dispute to SDSI as legal fees can very quickly mount when a disputant starts to claim data protection, bullying, defamation, etc. No matter how fair the board or their nominated disciplinary committee is, they may always be perceived as biased by the claimant. Claimants are also quick to seek a legal remedy. However they should have gone through the internal processes first. The advantage of not using the courts and going to the SDSI is that the process is:

• Quicker
• Cheaper
• Confidential
• Less formal
• Less damaging to relationships

The courts are generally against hearing sporting cases and adjudicating on personal sporting disputes. For instance in the selection dispute of *Jacob v Irish Amateur Rowing* Judge Laffoy stated it is 'pertinent to ask whether it is appropriate at all in the absence of proof of *mala fides* [bad faith] for a Court to intervene in a decision of an organisation governing a particular sport as to matters of selection and de-selection for competitive events.'[80] As Judge Smyth said in a 2007 case: 'Sports organisations do best to resolve differences under their own governing codes, rather than recourse to the courts of law.'[81]

The reluctance of the judiciary to get involved in sport may be summed up by Chief Justice Mr Frank Clarke: 'If every time a party was able to pass the relatively low threshold of suggesting that it had a legal case against a sporting body it is likely that the administration of major sports would grind to a halt.'[82]

Similarly, in *Dollingstown FC v IFA*[83] the judge commented that in-house tribunals are staffed by individuals with substantial knowledge of the particular sporting activity concerned. 'Such tribunals can generally provide the benefits of expert adjudication, speed and flexibility of resolution, cost and privacy.'

Facilities Management

Even small clubs may have a big investment in a club house or storage facility. These require maintenance, cleaning and insurance.

Sports Report

A board meeting is concerned overall with the sport and not operations or how the teams played. Clearly if there is ongoing poor performance that is a matter for the board but the emphasis of the board is on the strategic oversight of the organisation.

Any Other Business

The chair should be wary of allowing any other business (AOB) on the agenda. Board members should be able to give sufficient prior notice to ensure that an item is included on the agenda and any pre-reading is circulated in time. There are very few issues that come up a few hours before a meeting. AOB is a sign of poor meeting management. An alternative is to have Matters Arising at the start of the meeting and a decision taken if the matter is to be added to the agenda.

Notice of Meetings and Attendance

The form of notice for board meetings, if not set out in the constitution, should be agreed in the board's terms of reference. It is a good idea for the sporting entity to have a separate email account so that its business is not mixed with personal email. Board members should be aware of possible requests under data protection laws for access to an entity's correspondence. As an example, an aggrieved member can make a data request for all information held by the entity about them. This can cause tremendous difficulties if the entity's emails are mixed with personal emails. When a member leaves the board their email account should be deleted.

The secretary of the meeting should minute who attended each meeting and keep a record of attendance. Board members are expected to attend all meetings. If absence is unavoidable, they should inform the chair or the board secretary as soon as they are aware.

Each board member should study all board papers before the meeting. Reports should not be read out at a meeting. This avoids time being wasted at the meeting and allows time for full discussion. Reports should be prepared in accordance with a planned programme and include a short summary page which clearly indicates what action or input is required by the board.

THE ROLE OF THE CHAIR IN MEETINGS[84]

The chair controls the meeting. The success in running the board and therefore running the sporting entity is in the hands of the chair. If the chair is weak the governance of the entity is weakened. The chair is responsible for ensuring board discipline, that all reports are circulated and read in advance of the meeting and that meetings start and finish on time.

The chair allocates time to each agenda item and is responsible for ensuring that there is adequate time for the discussion of each item and that all board members participate. At the end of each agenda item the chair should state the decision and the action point to be minuted, or the resolution to be noted.

The chair must ensure that each board member is confident that they can offer their view in a respectful environment. Open debate should be encouraged and to ensure this, board members need to be sure of board confidentiality. If an individual has a lengthy point, they should be encouraged to put it in writing and for it to be circulated for consideration at a subsequent meeting. The chair must never allow a dominant individual to take control of the meeting.

A board is a collection of individuals and how they interact can determine the effectiveness of the board. Individuals may have no experience of the boardroom and may be unfamiliar with meeting etiquette. The behaviour of individuals results from their experience, their values and their understanding of where power and authority rest. The chair is there to facilitate mutual respect and enforce etiquette.

In any board there is always the risk of 'group think', i.e. where board members follow one another in the interests of harmony rather than critically evaluating and analysing an issue. Individuals may follow a leader who nominated them to the board. The chair is there to ensure that each board member thinks for themselves.

The chair allocates actions at a meeting, ensuring that the person responsible for the action point clearly understands it and is happy to take the responsibility. If this does not happen, at the next meeting it is likely that the person responsible will simply argue with the wording of the action point, particularly if they have not delivered the action on time.

UPDATES ON ACTIVITIES[85]

Depending on the size of the sport the board should get a regular update on activities and take decisions as to the next steps.

Ideally there should be a work plan for the year. The work to be completed during the year might include:

- Preparation or review of strategy and budgets
- Reviewing the financials
- Committee reports
- Reporting of key staff or volunteers
- Consideration of grants
- Governance reviews
- Monitoring of use of government or donor funds
- Annual strategy away day
- Specific issues, e.g. amalgamation of two affiliates
- Risk management, e.g. cyber risk
- Health and safety
- Safeguarding children, Garda vetting
- Update of policies, e.g. data protection
- Compliance with legal, regulatory and contractual obligations
- Work to be carried out by specific board members and/or committees
- Recruitment of new board members
- Training for the board, e.g. GDPR

Good meetings strengthen teamwork and camaraderie on the board. The chair needs to ensure that the focus is on strategic issues and not on operational matters, which may be very immediate and can tend to dominate discussion at meetings but are the responsibility of the executive.

Behaviour at Meetings

Poor behaviour at meetings may result from the passion people have for the sport, or competing factions or divisions, or simply people protecting their 'territory'. A strong chair does much to ensure that all have a role to play and that diversity of opinion, skill sets, experience and personalities are managed. Below are some common sources of conflict.

With Founder Members

Conflict may arise with founder members. They feel the entity is their own. They had a vision and brought it to life. The board can help the founders to move on by recognising their past achievements and listening to what they have to say.

If the founder is the chair it can be particularly difficult. Adopting appropriate policies to limit the ability of one individual or group to dominate rather than taking them on head to head may resolve the conflict. The constitution – and if a company, the duties under the Companies Act – must prevail.

If a decision is made for the founder and the entity to part, the board should investigate how to let the founder go with due respect for their work or how the board members can leave and hand over to new board members in an orderly fashion.

With the Executive

Conflicts between the executive and the board may occur. This is often caused by a lack of clarity over their respective roles and inadequate communication. Clear terms of reference, including delegated authority, need to be regularly reviewed, particularly in a growing entity. As an entity grows board members who were hands-on need to step back. Informal and social meetings of the board and the executive may help to diffuse frustration (see Chapter 9: The CEO – Roles and Responsibilities). Rotation of the board, with a few members retiring each year and no one staying beyond defined time limits, leads to changing approaches to the executive. Sports may also consider having set terms for senior executives.

With Factions

Factions can develop easily. Board members need to be reminded that they are bound by the decision of the board, even when they disagree, and they must work with integrity to carry out their responsibilities. The damage of conflict to the sport should be highlighted.

Inner circles are disruptive. The circle may be a purposeful attempt to exclude some board members or it may be a result of certain board members just being more proactive than others.

A skills analysis of the board may highlight the skills available and how best to use them. Decision-making processes and delegated authority must be clear to avoid dominance by one faction. There should be a clear code of conduct. Rotation of groups on tasks and on committees encourages camaraderie. Informal meetings and social occasions allow people to talk.

If a conflict becomes problematic the board should move quickly to mediation.

AFTER THE MEETING

Minutes[86]

Decisions of the board are recorded in minutes. They give a record of the meeting, setting out who was present, all appointments (if any) made, the proceedings and, in particular, the decisions taken at the meeting. The chair may choose how much of the discussion on an agenda item should be documented.

To encourage board members to participate freely it is recommended to minute the issue, the pertinent points, the decision as to what was agreed, why it was agreed, who took responsibility for it and the resulting actions. If a board member has concerns over a proposed action or about the running of the sporting entity, they can ask that their concerns are recorded. Board members should, however, remember that a decision of the board is a collective decision, even if they voted against the decision or voiced their concern in the boardroom.

At the following board meeting, the minutes are formally approved and signed by the chair. They should be filed in a register of minutes together with backing documentation.

The list of action points should be updated after each board meeting and clearly show who is responsible for an action and the date that action should be completed by.

Board minutes should be in a consistent format. Draft minutes should be approved by the chair and any actions circulated within five days of the meeting to allow all board members to work on their action points.

The board may consider publishing summary reports of board meetings in the interests of transparency.

Board members should use the minutes and the list of action points to start working immediately on the tasks for which they are responsible, and not two or so days, or hours, before the next meeting.

Access to Advice[87]

The chair or company secretary should ensure that board members have reasonable access to independent legal or financial advice. This is particularly important if there are solvency issues.

CULTURE

Those who promote governance codes purport to show how to avoid governance failures. Most of the recommendations in codes are structural – controls, policies, committees. However, the culture of an organisation is crucial. It is important that a board builds a level of openness and trust. It is useful for the board members to spend informal time together, for instance over a meal, to allow for the informal exchange of ideas.

Board members need to be encouraged to express their dissent. Mavericks and dissenters can be trying but they are not disloyal. Silent board members need to be encouraged to speak. Group think is dangerous. By meeting formally and informally in different environments and in different combinations board members can learn to respect each other and share and challenge difficult information.

Away days, whether to discuss strategy or enjoy their sport, are useful for board members and the executive to get to know each other as people.

A key reason for volunteers to join a board is out of interest and enjoyment of the sport. No matter how intense a discussion this objective is key.

THE SMALLER ENTITY

The principle of ensuring that the board exercises its collective responsibility through board meetings that are efficient and effective is particularly important in smaller entities. A strong chair is essential to ensure that notice is given of meetings, that meetings start and finish on time, that all get to express their views and that minutes are taken.[88]

The board should make sure that someone is appointed (usually called a secretary) to keep track of the group's records, meeting minutes, membership, and so on.[89]

Potential conflicts with founder members may occur. There is also the danger of small groups developing. The chair can work to allot tasks across different groups to reduce the emergence of factions.

In the case of disputes ensure that internal procedures are followed and act quickly. Small club cases can quickly escalate, e.g. Thomas Talbot's defamation case against Hermitage Golf Club, which took 83 days in the High and Supreme Courts. Talbot was an amateur golfer who claimed he was falsely accused of cheating about his handicap.[90] The courts are not the place to resolve sporting issues, but this does not stop claimants and their lawyers from taking this route.

The cultural and social aspect is an important part of sporting life in smaller entities as well as large organisations.

CONCLUSION

Running an effective meeting is a skilled task and this is the role of the chair. There is an etiquette to meetings, and the chair should insist on discipline to ensure an effective meeting and should be supported by all board members.

The next chapter considers board activities, and in particular ensuring the development of the board.

Ten Key Points

1. There should be a plan of the year's board meetings so that time is not wasted at meetings setting dates.
2. The chair and the board secretary prepare the agenda. Board members and the executive should ask the chair if they want an item included.
3. Consideration of the list of action points is important in the preparation of the agenda.
4. The agenda and board meeting must be circulated at least three days before the meeting.
5. Details of how to run board meetings may be laid out in the constitution or the terms of reference of the board.
6. The role of chair is critical to the running of a disciplined board meeting.
7. The chair should ensure that all board members can air their opinion and at the same time be wary of group think.
8. Informal and social occasions may bring greater board cohesion. Away days can be very useful. If there are irreconcilable differences the board should move quickly to a decision or mediation.
9. Board minutes should be in a consistent format. Draft minutes should be approved by the chair and circulated within five days of the meeting to allow all board members to work on their action points.
10. Board members should remember that a decision of the board is a collective decision, even if they voted against the decision or voiced their concern in the boardroom.

5

BOARD MEMBER ACTIVITIES

- Introduction
- Recruitment and Succession
- Development and Evaluation of the Board
- Board Size
- Length of Service – Board Members
- Leaving the Board
- The Smaller Entity
- Conclusion
- Ten Key Points

INTRODUCTION

For a sporting entity to work effectively it needs a competent board. This can be achieved by continually reviewing recruitment, training and rotation processes. A key challenge is that many sporting people and entities are resistant to having people leading their entity who are not from the sport. However, as sport becomes more professional, as stakeholders demand better governance and as the money in sport increases, the need for a board that is run along professional lines increases.

If an entity is being run professionally this means that board members are chosen to fill gaps in competencies on the board, that training is made available, that the performance of the board and the board members are evaluated, and that there is an orderly handover on succession.

RECRUITMENT AND SUCCESSION[91]

Board members recruited to the board must have the interests of the sport at heart. It is essential that board members do not bring their personal agendas to their role and are prepared to work as part of a team.

The Sports Code requires that recruitment must involve reviewing the mix of skills and experience on the board and considering diversity of background and experience. It asks that the board should be made up of member representatives, athletes, trainers, independent voices, and/or external representatives to avoid loyalty dilemmas. Loyalty dilemmas can be extremely difficult, particularly if there are coaches or selectors on the board or a person in charge of funding.

There remain considerable obstacles for any sporting entity to ensure that their board has a balanced mix of skills, experience and independence. It may be difficult without external influence to change an entity's constitution to allow a balanced mix that promotes equal opportunities and diversity.

The Skills of a Balanced Board

The board needs to strike a balance between those who have a detailed or expert knowledge of the sport and those, possibly from outside the sport, who have a professional skill set. Ideally a board requires a mix of board members who have business experience and in-depth knowledge of the sport.

Relevant experience may include:

- Administration
- Financial
- Legal
- Governance
- Marketing/commercial
- Risk management
- Board experience
- Business management
- Communications/PR
- Human resource management

At present the Sports Code, unlike the UK Code for Sports Governance, does not insist on external board members. As a result, there is a danger that board members are selected not on the basis of their competence but on their sporting involvement, power or popularity.

Sports may struggle to identify suitably qualified people from outside the sport to sit on the board. Board members may worry that the sport itself might suffer if governed by non-sporting people or perhaps even fear the loss of privileges associated with their position. But a balanced board leads to better decision-making and better performance of the board.

Accessing specific skills externally can be expensive, particularly for a small club. It can be more cost-effective to have professional people on the board. For example, having professional finance people on the board is a protection against the dangers of financial difficulties.

For transparency, information on the professional background of board members should be published together with conflicts of interest and information on other positions in sports organisations held by that board member.

Generally, the constitution defines how a person is chosen to sit on the board. Some positions may be via election; others via selection, representation or nomination. Common conditions include a representative from each region and that any board member must be a paid-up member of the sport. It is easy to argue that no one outside the sport is likely to agree to be a volunteer board member. Conversely, professional people may be happy to volunteer but only if they believe the entity is genuinely committed to good governance.

In order to provide for more independent directors, it is wise to have a governance committee consider the matter, propose changes to the constitution to the board and then engage in a series of meetings with clubs or regions regarding the proposals which would be put forward at the next AGM.

Elections

Many board members in sporting entities are elected by ballot by the membership. Sporting entities are advised to ensure a clear election policy is set out in their constitution and the eligibility criteria and timelines are fair and transparent, and issued to the membership well in advance of candidacy deadlines. Many disputes in sporting entities arise around how elections are managed and held, and many abuses of dominant positions within sporting entities find their power in the failure to have open and transparent electoral procedures.

Those elected onto positions on the board should have to stand for re-election every two to four years by the membership with a maximum term limit. A sporting entity should also consider who is eligible to run for election – members should not be unnecessarily fettered in terms of putting their candidacy forward, however the entity should consider how they can bring a mix of skills onto the board. This may mean changing rules to ensure at least one position be reserved for candidates with financial or legal skills for example, or may require the entity to co-opt additional individuals onto the board with such skills after the elected positions have been filled.

It can be difficult to change these rules, even if they are manifestly unfair or archaic, as a 75 per cent majority in companies is required and even in unincorporated entities a 66 per cent or 75 per cent level is often required to change the constitution. One common discussion is whether a small sport or region should have the same vote as a large sport or region.

Whatever the rules for elections, the board must ensure that the rules are followed. It can be useful to have an acting lawyer or accountant in attendance.

Diversification

Sport is big business. Boards need people who understand business and how to run an entity. The National Sports Policy highlights that 'it is also important to consider the issue of women in leadership positions including as NGB Board members and CEOs'[92] and seeks for NGBs to 'be asked to set gender diversity targets and develop equality action plans.'[93] There has been a lot of discussion and debate around quotas but there is consensus that a diverse board and the inclusion of more women create better boards. Some NGBs have inserted gender equality quotas and/or gender balancing objectives into their board and election candidacy criteria.

Change is coming and there are an increasing number of women in leadership positions. This is supported by Sport Ireland's Women in Sport initiative and a new strategic plan. Many sporting organisations are now investing in women's leadership programmes and specific gender equality programmes for membership.

The board, when looking at recruitment, development and succession, must ensure that equality and diversification are considered. This not only relates to gender issues but also to disability, race and economic backgrounds.

Succession

Recruitment is linked with succession. The constitution usually sets out rules for the election of new board members. Where board members are nominated by members and elected from the floor this can lead to a severe skills gap on the board. This can be extremely difficult to rectify due to vested interests. The issue should be discussed at board level. Perhaps consultants can be co-opted to advise or attend board or committee meetings. The membership should be made aware and the issue addressed at least gradually as board members rotate. An examination of the skills required by the board, the preparation of a job description and circulation among the members on a timely basis should lead to appointments being made on merit relating to the skills shortage. Even where board members are representatives, the skills they bring to the board should be critical to their selection.

DEVELOPMENT AND EVALUATION OF THE BOARD[94]

Professional Development

The Sports Code recommends appropriate training for board members in larger sporting entities. At least annually the board should consider its competencies and diversification. The Sports Code also looks for the effectiveness of the board, the committees and the board members to be assessed.

Continual professional development is a requirement of most professions. Gaps in knowledge should be identified on recruitment and induction and clear steps taken to help the board member address these shortcomings. Such gaps might be in basic board skills such as understanding the Sports Code or the financials. It should also cover the sport and changes in the rules of the sport and health and safety issues arising, e.g. concussion. Training should be appropriate and aimed at filling competency gaps on the board. As governance relates to running an entity, training in governance should be a high priority.

Evaluation

The board should undertake an annual review of its own effectiveness and that of its committees. Evaluation leads to the clearer definition of roles and an understanding of responsibilities. It highlights the strengths and weaknesses of the board. A well-run evaluation serves to motivate board members and identify training or development required.

Where there are terms of reference for the board as a whole and for individual members the board and the members should evaluate their performance against the terms of reference. This will highlight gaps in skills. It may also lead to improving terms of reference.

Any evaluation of performance may be resisted by volunteer board members who may consider that the entity should be thankful for anything they do. Even a professional board may be hesitant to organise board evaluations. The procedure of evaluation may be unnerving as it is not something that they are familiar with. They may argue that it is a waste of time. The National Sports Governance Observer reports that a governance principle that scores lowest is 'organising board self-evaluations'.[95]

The process of evaluation might look at measurement against the strategic plan and the board's communication with members and stakeholders. The chair might meet informally with each board member and ask for feedback on meetings and how the board member feels they can contribute. Alternatively, each member might be asked to complete a form evaluating the performance of the board against their terms of reference and strategy. It can be useful to have an external facilitator as they will be seen to be independent.

The points raised at evaluation can then be discussed at a subsequent meeting. Board evaluation is a useful tool in internal accountability and control.

Board Size

The constitution or terms of reference of the board may set out the board size and composition. The board should be an appropriate size so that it can be an effective decision-making organ. There is no right size but a board of seven to nine people is a good working size. A smaller team is more flexible and can react quickly. It also allows all members to contribute at meetings without undue loss of time. Large boards, for instance of more than twelve people, are unwieldy and therefore inefficient and should be discouraged.

It is common for former large boards to be re-organised into a small board and a larger council. The terms of reference of the council need to be carefully set out and explained and agreed. The role of the council can be varied and will depend on the entity and the re-organisation. The role may perhaps be operational, perhaps as overseer of the rules of the sport or perhaps as guardian of the values of the organisation. Council members may be relieved to no longer have the legal responsibilities of a board member.

Length of Service – Board Members

There should be clear term limits for how long a member can serve on a board. These limits may be set out in the constitution or in the terms of reference. Term limits allow the sport to refresh the board with new faces and talents. This must be balanced with the potential loss of experience and knowledge, particularly in a smaller sport. Term limits of six to nine years are considered reasonable. In a sport with a small pool of experienced board members, it may be suitable to ask a board member to stand down for a year or two before putting themselves back for election.

The question of term limits for a CEO in sporting organisations is divisive. The danger of having no rotation may result in considerable power being accumulated in this position. Regular performance reviews of the CEO by a strong board may mitigate this risk. The board should consider carefully the employment contract and term on appointment of a CEO.

LEAVING THE BOARD

A board member may leave the board on rotation or they may wish to resign. What is important is that the handover is orderly. This means leaving a list of work in progress and important issues. If a board member wishes to resign, they do not immediately absolve themselves from liabilities. For instance, if a sporting entity is in financial difficulty, a liquidator will look into all transactions in the previous year.

A board member may wish to resign over a particular issue about which they feel strongly. In this case they should write a letter to the board for the board to consider. It is for the chair to decide whether to invite the board member to a board meeting to discuss the issue.

In extreme circumstances the whole board may wish to resign, possibly as a result of conflict with management or following a public crisis or request from membership to step down. Even still the board should work to achieve an orderly handover, ensuring that they hand over the affairs to new board members rather than leaving no board member in place. The board members have a duty to the entity and it reflects badly on the departing board members if they leave the entity without leadership.

The board may wish to remove a board member. The constitution may have clauses in it for such a removal. However it is strongly recommended that due process is followed to the letter and that legal advice is sought. Not only may there be employment issues involved but the board member may counter with allegations of discrimination, defamation or GDPR issues. It may be appropriate to ask the board member to stand aside or, if paid, to take garden leave, until the issues are settled. The duty of confidentiality remains after resignation.

THE SMALLER ENTITY

Even a smaller entity should continually review recruitment, development and retirement processes to ensure relevant competencies are in place.[96] This may mean seeking to put a lawyer, an accountant or a computer expert on the board. Board members should agree as to who they would like to invite onto the board, bearing in mind the need for a mix of skills and diversity in terms of background and experience.[97] At least once a year the members should look at how the working of the board could be improved.[98]

Training is important in small entities as well as large ones. Training in safeguarding children, health and safety, and data protection should be prioritised. The death of Benjamin Robinson from a fatal brain injury playing rugby with his school highlights the risks that can be involved in local sport.[99]

Having appropriate rules in the constitution or in a board member's contract or letter of appointment for the departure or removal of a board member is important.

CONCLUSION[100]

Boards need to be aware of the importance of a diverse, professional and well-run board. Effective recruitment, training and rotation are key. The board and the members need to assess the strength of their board and even whether their constitution should be changed to allow a more balanced board. Evaluation of the board, both internally and by external consultants, is an excellent tool for ensuring a strong board.

Part III considers the key roles of the board – strategy, risk, accountability and monitoring.

Ten Key Points

1. Every entity should have a clear and formal process for the appointment of new board members to the board.
2. All board appointments should be made on merit with regard to the skills required on the board as well as being in line with the constitution.

3. The board should ensure continual professional development.
4. When recruiting to a board the membership should consider diversification.
5. A board member must have adequate time available to contribute to their role. Famous names can look good but if they are only a figurehead this simply increases the burden on other board members.
6. Evaluation of the board should concentrate on knowledge and achievement of strategy, the balance of skills and knowledge, diversity and the ability of the board to work effectively as a collective.
7. Evaluation should be aimed at motivating the board members.
8. The evaluation of each board member is to determine if they contribute effectively to the board.
9. There should be clear term limits. Term limits allow the sport to refresh the board with new faces and talents. This must be balanced with the potential loss of experience and knowledge.
10. On leaving the board, even if it is an acrimonious resignation, the board member should aim for an orderly handover.

Part III

The Board – Strategy, Risk, Accountability, Monitoring

6

STRATEGY

- Introduction
- The Need for a Strategy
- The Constitution
- Vision and Mission
- The Strategic Plan
- Budgets
- Measuring Success and Key Performance Indicators
- Stakeholders and External Influencers
- The Smaller Entity
- Conclusion
- Ten Key Points

INTRODUCTION

Why is strategy so important? It shows how the objectives of the entity are to be fulfilled. It is the plan for the running of the sport. It is the road map for the organisation. In a larger organisation the board members delegate the implementation of the strategy to the executive, and the board members monitor its work.

This chapter looks at the steps necessary to build a strategy. Its creation needs to be a team effort to ensure that all parties 'buy in'. Ideally all board members, committees, staff, volunteers and the membership have an opportunity to contribute. Team engagement events such as an 'away' day are an excellent way of bringing all together and increasing social cohesion. External consultants can also assist sporting entities in the preparation of the strategic plan.

THE NEED FOR A STRATEGY

Sport Ireland requires sight of a strategy for any sporting entity receiving funding, so many larger organisations will have a strategic plan in place. However, the majority of small sporting entities do not have a written strategy. They continue along their annual timetable with certain events throughout the year and maybe one or two national competitions and some training for elite athletes. Their strategy may simply be to do the same thing every year.

What if the sport wants to grow? Are they interested in catering for people with a disability or in responding to the huge rise in women's sports? Do they want to raise standards, increase training or to give more support to their elite athletes? Do they want sponsorship? Are their sponsors looking for better governance? Are they seeking funding from Sport Ireland? If so, they need a strategy.

A good example is the National Sports Policy, which sets out 57 actions that are to be achieved over ten years. From this overall plan, annual objectives are set, business plans agreed and key performance indicators (KPIs) (see below in this chapter) are set to measure implementation. It is the board's role to ensure that there are adequate resources to fulfil the plan. The board will consider the annual objectives, create an annual operational plan and budget and then break that down further into individual tasks. The figure below shows how a strategic plan is translated into individual tasks.

Figure 1: From Strategic Plan to Individual Task

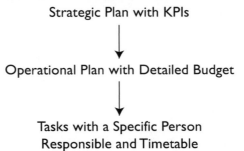

Strategic Plan with KPIs

Operational Plan with Detailed Budget

Tasks with a Specific Person
Responsible and Timetable

THE CONSTITUTION

When preparing a strategy, the first step is to consider the purpose of the sporting entity. The purpose, or objects, of an entity are set out in the constitution or founding document (see Chapter 3: The Constitution). The strategic plan must follow these objectives as they are the reason for the existence of that entity. In an incorporated entity if the board members believe that the objectives should be changed then they have to have an extraordinary general meeting (see Chapter 8: General Meetings) and 75 per cent of the membership must vote in favour. This is because they are changing the purpose of the entity.

An example of a sporting entity's objectives is set out in the Badminton Union of Ireland's constitution:

'The main object for which the Company is established is to be the governing body of the game of Badminton in the Republic of Ireland and Northern Ireland (hereafter together referred to as 'Ireland') and to control, advance, promote, foster and safeguard the interests of the Game in Ireland and the doing of all other such things as are incidental or conducive to the attainment of the above object.'[101]

The constitution then goes on to list ancillary powers, e.g. to raise money, but these can only be exercised in promoting the main object.

Every entity should have its objectives in its constitution. These objectives should be the backbone of any strategy.

VISION AND MISSION[102]

Once the objectives have been clarified the sporting entity needs to develop its vision and mission in line with those objectives.

The vision statement is an aspirational statement to motivate those involved in the sport. The mission succinctly explains the role of the entity and how it plans to attain its vision. In formulating the vision the board members should ask themselves what do they want this entity to look like in future. The mission should be based on the founding document of the entity. The strategic plan for the Irish Rugby Football Union (IRFU) is a good example of an entity's vision and mission:

The IRFU vision: 'Irish Rugby: Building success, together'

The IRFU mission is:

'To develop and grow the game through:

- Excellence in performance
- Quality experiences
- Effective engagement
- Great people
- Strong leadership'[103]

In any plan the values of the entity need to be identified. Ethical leadership comes from the top. The IRFU puts its values right at the beginning of its strategic plan:

- Respect
- Integrity

- Inclusivity
- Fun
- Excellence

THE STRATEGIC PLAN[104]

The strategic plan sets out the:

- Goals to achieve the vision and mission
- Actions to achieve those goals
- Milestones and indicators for measuring progress in achieving those goals

The strategy of a national governing body (NGB) should cascade down to its affiliates and clubs. This is well illustrated in the GAA Strategic Plan 2018–2021:[105]

'1. The GAA Strategic Plan 2018–2021 represents the "big picture" strategic priorities of the GAA and is geared towards the overall development of the Association.
2. Strategic Plans devised by provinces, counties and clubs link to priorities in the organisation-wide plan, but are also tailored to local issues.
3. Operational Plans by central committees and work departments are positioned to implement the core activities and plans of the Association.'

The GAA then focuses its strategy on specific goals:

- Games participation
- Volunteer and administration growth
- Governance and administration
- Communication
- Protection and growth[106]

And sets out the specific tasks to be pursued to achieve these goals.

The strategy of the Olympic Federation of Ireland is a good example. It divides its strategic plan into five pillars:

- Putting athletes first
- Enabling performance
- Inspiring Ireland
- Becoming financially independent
- Operating to the highest standards

The aim of the plan is to allow the OFI 'to be laser focused on preparing and leading our nation's finest competitors at the Summer, Winter and Youth Olympic World and European Games'.[107]

Contents of a Strategic Plan

A strategic plan might include:

- Introduction and context
- Vision and mission
- Values
- Strategic objectives
- Key actions to achieve these objectives
- Financing
- Risks to be managed
- High-level implementation plan

Improving governance and additional training for board members, staff or volunteers should also be part of the plan.

An example of a well-laid-out strategic plan is that of Badminton Ireland,[108] which presents its plans across its eight business areas:

- Membership services
- Tournaments and events
- Volunteering
- High performance
- Governance
- Finance

- Marketing
- ICT (Information and communications technology)

In the Badminton Ireland document, each section has an overview, the strategic objectives and measurable outcomes, with the person or department responsible identified and a clear timetable.

High Performance

The Rio Review[109] of the 2016 Olympics by Sport Ireland highlighted that there is room for a more strategic approach and for further enhancements in the high-performance system. Funding and governance were identified as key in improving high performance. Strategy should look at a multi-cycle approach, identify medal targets, attracting funding and governance in relation to any high-performance committee.

Finances

A strategy ideally should include high-level projections of income versus expenditure, and funding over the period of the strategy. It is common for sporting entities to prepare a separate budget for internal use but their publicised strategic plan does not address financial objectives. While it is acknowledged that giving financial objectives and projections is not common practice at present, for better transparency it would be preferable if entities make more financial planning information available to their members. This is particularly relevant to entities that have debt or other external sources of funding.

Running the finances of the sporting entity is an integral part of the work of the whole board. The board, on reviewing a strategic plan, must review the related budgets and underlying assumptions.

Cricket Ireland is a good example of an entity that addresses financial objectives in their strategic plan:[110]

- 'Securing a new broadcast agreement making this our single largest commercial source of income

- Expanding our sponsorship portfolio and adding value to our commercial partners to best in class standards
- Increasing other self-generated income including events, merchandising, online activities and other revenue streams
- Controlling fixed costs to ensure that they remain within the parameters of fixed funding
- Building minimum cash reserves equivalent to 12 months operating costs
- Introducing a financial and budgetary reporting model for Provincial Unions under new service level agreements.'

Review

The overall strategy should be reviewed after two to three years or if any significant change in circumstances takes place, for instance to assess the impact of the 2020 coronavirus pandemic. Strategic issues should be part of the annual board plan of work and ideally examined and measured on a quarterly basis. In larger organisations where the strategy may be drafted by the executive or with the aid of consultants, the role of the board is to challenge constructively and contribute to its development and to approve the final document. The board, not the executive nor the consultants, is responsible for the resulting strategic plan and on-going reviews.

Implementing the Plan[111]

To implement the strategic plan, it needs to be broken down into a list of actions that are then delegated to specific individuals or groups. Usually the operational plan is set annually or in annual periods with timelines, targets, budgets and funding actions detailed and allocated to individuals or committees. By setting milestones and targets the performance of those individuals and groups can be measured. This operational plan ensures that all are working as a team and key priorities are identified. This, in turn, allows better use of time and resources. As part of the plan written policies may be developed, e.g. altering the terms of reference for volunteers to include training.

The strategic plan of the Irish Athletic Boxing Association explains the relationship between its strategic plan and its operational plan:[112]

'The plan will be supported by an annual operational plan. This operational plan will be prepared by the CEO and approved by the Board in conjunction with preparing annual budgets. This operational plan will take each of the actions and set out clearly:

1. Who is responsible for each action
2. Specific details of how each action will be implemented
3. How each action will be measured for success through key performance indicators
4. Detailed timetables and milestones for each action and each of the overall goals
5. Budgets required and potential revenue streams
6. Resources required to achieve each action'

A timetable helps the board members monitor the implementation of the specific actions. Changes, both within the entity and externally, may cause amendments to be made in the plan. As a result, the operational plan needs to be reviewed approximately every three months to ensure that the actions are achievable and can be accomplished in the given time frame. This is particularly important if, for example, an expected source of funding does not materialise.

For a plan to be successful it needs to be accepted by those who implement it. If the plan is seen as being forced from the top it is likely that it will be resisted. Those responsible for individual tasks usually have a better idea as to the resources and time necessary to achieve a task and should be consulted during the preparation and review of the plan. They will be much more supportive and take ownership of the actions if this process has taken place.

The funding of any sport is critical to any plan. Therefore, the operational plan should include contact with funders/sponsors, grant applications and fundraising activities.

It is the role of the board to monitor and evaluate the implementation of the plan. They need to ensure that there are sufficient resources in the form of time, funding, volunteers and employees to implement the strategy. If there is a shortfall, for instance of funding, the board members will need to review the strategic plan. Where there are financial problems it is their duty to consider the sustainability of the entity.

The implementation of the plan will be broken into different areas. For instance, the OFI divides its operations into 'business domains',[113] including:

- *Games operation:* logistics, insurance, NGB liaison
- *Sports operations:* accreditations, compliance, kit, data capture, anti-doping, integrity, child welfare, athlete welfare, pre-games training camps
- *High-performance planning:* sport science and medical support structures, support to athletes and coaches, athletes' and coaches' charters, medicals, nutrition, environmental reporting, performance tracking
- *Athlete support:* athlete outreach and welfare, education and support workshops, schools outreach programme
- *Funding and grants:* support programmes, team preparation grants, scholarships
- *Commercial and marketing:* sponsorship, market research, ticketing compliance, merchandising, advertising
- *Communications:* media operations, social media communications, brand management
- *Finance:* grant applications, reporting

BUDGETS[114]

The budget is simply the plan expressed in figures. A high-level budget should be prepared to cover the strategic plan and more detailed budgets should be prepared to support the operational plans for each year.

During the year the executive compares the actual results with the budget and with prior year results. This shows how it is progressing against its budget and can be seen by the board as a control or an indicator as to how well the executive is performing. It should be noted that time put into the budget is an ineffective use of management time if subsequent comparisons to budget simply highlight a poor budget rather than good or poor performance.

Budgeting and monitoring finances are a fundamental part of the work of the board. Finances should be reviewed at every meeting or at least quarterly. This is particularly important as many sporting entities are under-funded. The annual budget should highlight periods when cash may be tight – for instance before annual membership fees come in. Board members must be aware that they must not trade if they cannot pay their suppliers. This is described as trading recklessly and board members can be held personally liable.

MEASURING SUCCESS AND KEY PERFORMANCE INDICATORS[115]

In addition to performance against budget, key performance indicators (KPIs) are useful to measure success. These are figures, percentages or ratios and highlight in a succinct way an entity's performance.

As an example, KPIs might include:

- Two players qualified for Olympics
- One Paralympic medal
- 10 per cent net increase in members
- Financial reserves equivalent to one year of costs

In any plan a specific person or a department should be identified as responsible for delivering or reporting on a particular KPI. The importance of KPIs is not the figure itself but to investigate the reasons why the KPI was not achieved or in some cases overachieved. For instance, is the high increase in members being set off by many members leaving? If so, why are so many members leaving and what can be done to encourage them to remain as members.

Budgets and KPIs set milestones as to when certain targets should be achieved. Not everything can be achieved in the first year and therefore timelines and rolling operational plans are necessary to drive priorities.

As Cricket Ireland says:

'These rolling operational plans will have detailed targets, budgets and resources allocated to enable delivery. ... We will maintain flexibility to "tweak" the plan based on changing circumstances and regularly review progress to ensure we remain on track to deliver the broad range of outcomes set out within this strategy.'[116]

The board's role is to monitor strategy. Discussions of performance against strategy should be a regular board agenda item. Some financial knowledge is crucial in this role. Board members should seek training if they are uncomfortable doing this.

STAKEHOLDERS AND EXTERNAL INFLUENCERS[117]

Stakeholders' Role in Strategy

When developing a strategy it is important to consider the interests of all stakeholders and external influencers. A sporting entity is dependent on many stakeholders. Sports are particularly exposed to external influence. A stakeholder is 'a person or group with an interest (a stake) in the actions or policies of an organisation, which means they may affect the actions or policies and/or be affected by them.'[118] If an entity is a national governing body (NGB) an important influencer is Sport Ireland. If the entity is lower in the pyramid, then the NGB may exert considerable influence.

When preparing the plan, it can be helpful if the entity consults with the stakeholders. If significant changes are planned, then active communication with all stakeholders and particularly all members is essential. The plan should also consider compliance with regulators.

Key Stakeholders

Key stakeholders may include:

- Members
- Elite athletes
- NGBs
- Government/local authorities
- Donors/sponsors
- Commercial entities

The Members (Including Participants and Athletes)

A successful sporting entity, like a successful business, should treat its members like customers. To keep coming back they must have a positive experience. All sports clubs need to both attract new members and retain existing ones. It is not only about marketing the entity and boasting of its achievements but also about listening to the members and offering the service that they are asking for.

Elite Athletes

The views of elite athletes must be heard and reflected in the strategy of the entity. It is useful if there is a regular consultation process where athletes can make representations to the board. Elite athletes can lose contact with their local club as they are competing at international level and organised by the sport's

NGB. However elite athletes remain powerful influencers at the local level.

National Governing Bodies

By keeping close links with the NGB local sporting entities can participate in the decisions as to how their sport is run. For instance, the NGB may be involved in investigating standards for protective helmets or other equipment.

Government/Local Authorities

Government policy towards sport decides a significant portion of funds available. These are generally distributed through Sport Ireland to the NGBs. There are certain exceptions where other government departments play a significant role, for instance the Department of Agriculture contributes a considerable part of the budget of Horse Sport Ireland (because of the horse-breeding aspect).

Local authorities play an important role in the provision of community sport and bring schools, clubs, NGBs and private entities together to create partnerships and improve delivery of sport to the community.

Donors/Sponsors

Sporting entities need to have a clear relationship with their donors. The entity must fulfil the terms of sponsorship/donation if they accept the funds. This may involve detailed negotiations of what exactly is involved and what, if any, perks or consideration the sponsor receives in return as well as discussions of other sponsors, exclusivity, ambush marketing, etc. Each sponsor or grantor has its own conditions. For example, a club may receive monies from different funds within a local authority – perhaps one grant for development of community sport and another as part of a fund resulting from the building of a dump or road nearby. Each will have its own conditions. Monies received from government or local authorities normally require a tax clearance certificate.

Commercial Entities

The strategy will also consider alternatives sources of funding, for instance commercialisation of sporting rights or the sale of branded kit.

THE SMALLER ENTITY

Vision, Mission and Strategic Plan

The strategy of a small sporting entity may be simply to continue running the annual competition schedule that they do each year. However it is useful for the board to discuss and agree the vision, mission, values and objectives of the entity and make sure that they remain relevant. The board should discuss how the group wants to achieve its objectives and how it wants to work.[119] The objectives should reflect the constitution.

The board should develop, resource, monitor and evaluate the plan so that the club achieves its stated purpose and objectives. Ideally every year the club agrees and writes down a plan which includes:

- The most important actions to meet objectives
- Timelines to achieve these actions
- Breakdown of the budget
- A description of how the money will be raised[120]

The board should agree who is going to take responsibility for the actions to carry out the plan,[121] review the plan once a year and have a discussion about what went well and what could be improved before agreeing a new work plan.[122]

The objectives of the club should be reviewed at least every three years.[123] The board should design policies around the plan as to how they want things to work.[124]

CONCLUSION

A carefully prepared strategic plan is a useful document that promotes an entity, highlights its professionality and sets out the work of the organisation according to its objectives for the next three to ten years.

Ten Key Points

1. The strategic plan must be in line with the purpose of the entity as set out in the constitution.
2. The vision statement is an aspirational statement motivating the sporting entity, while the mission succinctly explains the role of the entity and how it plans to attain its vision.
3. The board should identify the values of the entity.
4. The strategic plan sets out:
   - the goals to achieve the vision and mission
   - the actions to achieve those goals
   - milestones and indicators for measuring progress in achieving those goals
5. For implementation the strategic plan is broken down into an operational plan, being a list of specific actions which are then delegated to specific individuals or groups.
6. It is the role of the board to monitor and evaluate the implementation of the strategy and operational plan.
7. The budget is simply the plan expressed in figures. Budgets and the monitoring of the finances is a fundamental part of running a sporting entity.
8. Key performance indicators (KPIs) are used to measure success. These may be percentages or ratios and highlight in a succinct way the entity's performance.

9. The entity should consult stakeholders during strategic planning and actively seek feedback.
10. If significant changes are planned the entity needs a careful consultation process with key stakeholders, particularly the members and funders.

7

RISK

- Introduction
- Understanding Risk Management
- Understanding the Accounts
- Systems and Controls
- Role of External Auditor
- Role of Internal Auditors and the Audit Committee
- Insurance
- Risks Associated with Not Incorporating
- Disaster Recovery/Continuity Plans
- The Smaller Entity
- Conclusion
- Ten Key Points

INTRODUCTION

This chapter looks at risk. It is important for sporting entities to discuss the risks they face. Risk management is not only for entities involved in relatively high-risk activities, e.g. cave diving or motor racing. It is a wide area covering, for example, financial, reputational, physical, and health and safety issues. Risk can be as simple as considering the likelihood of a person tripping and falling on entering a room. A vital area is the protection of minors. Sadly, this is still an area that requires considerable attention.

This chapter considers how board members can mitigate risk by good financial reporting and implementing systems and controls. It looks at how the primary role of the external auditor is not to look for fraud but to report on the figures to the members. On the other hand, the board, who are ultimately responsible, can use the internal auditor or the audit committee to ensure that risk is minimised.

Insurance is important in the mitigation of risk and this chapter considers various types of insurance that a sporting entity might have. Insurance for some sporting entities may be seen as a substitute for incorporating. This is true to some extent, but incorporation gives better protection from liability and may lead to better governance as a result of the requirements of the Companies Act.

Finally, the chapter touches on disaster recovery in case the worst happens.

UNDERSTANDING RISK MANAGEMENT[125]

The first step in risk management is to do a risk assessment of the sporting entity. This means making a list of all the risks that the entity might face. At least once a year the board members should discuss these risks, making sure that everyone understands them.

The amount of risk that an entity and its members tolerate varies from entity to entity. The board should discuss their risk appetite. How much risk is the entity prepared to accept in achieving its objectives?

Types of Risk

There are many different types of risks that a sport can be exposed to. These include:

- *Financial risks:* for example, liquidity risk where the entity does not have funds available when needed. What is the chance that their sources of funding will dry up? What steps can they take? Soccer clubs provide an example where several have struggled to meet wages while some have ceased to operate completely.[126]
- *Strategic risk:* what might stop the sporting entity achieving its strategic objectives – lack of funding, loss of reputation? The Olympic Federation of Ireland completely revised its strategy to focus on athletes first following the Rio crisis of 2016.
- *Operational risks:* for example, accidents, theft, fire, or health and safety concerns.
- *Force majeure:* where an issue beyond the control of the club impacts it. For example, Magheracloone Gaelic Football Club in Co. Monaghan was forced to shut after its playing fields subsided following the collapse of an underground mine.
- *Membership risk:* what might cause membership to fall? What actions can be taken? For example, there has been a significant decline in young people taking up golf[127] and also the recession impacted membership of sports that are perceived as expensive or with high membership fees, e.g. sailing and gym membership.
- *Information and technological risks:* this might include identity theft and breach of data protection regulations. It may be as simple, for example, as an email intended for the

management team on the strengths and weaknesses of players being accidentally sent to all players.

- *Brand and reputational risks:* what factors could lead to reputational damage? For example, a sportsperson mistreats an animal while competing or there is a severe injury to a minor. How can this be anticipated, managed and controlled? For example, the Irish Amateur Swimming Association's reputation was damaged in 1998 when Derek O'Rourke, a former national and Olympic swimming coach, was found guilty of sexually abusing young female swimmers. The new organisation, Swim Ireland, has worked tirelessly to restore trust with a comprehensive child welfare policy.
- *Human resource risks:* an example would be where too much power is in the hands of one individual, or there is a lack of succession planning.
- *Tax compliance:* for example this may involve flouting PAYE rules with salary payments made in cash.
- *Accounting:* are controls in place to ensure that true and fair records are being kept? Or does one person bank the cash and keep the records and receive the bank statements, leaving the entity exposed to potential fraud? Regular back-ups of databases and the accounts are essential. If an accounting system cannot be backed up as the programme is internet-based (on the cloud) then a full suite of reports should be printed at regular intervals.

This list is not exhaustive. Risk can come from many areas, for instance a decision of government or an NGB or that of a supranational organisation, e.g. discussions on disbanding a club or province or the postponement of events.

Reducing Risk

Once a sport has compiled a list of potential risks and the risks are understood, the board members need to discuss how to manage them. The board may decide to:

- Avoid a risk by not allowing it to occur. For example, preventing the use of a hazardous exit with poor visibility from a sports complex. Another example would be making a rule change to outlaw certain behaviours (e.g. gambling/racism).
- Reduce the risk by training and education and making staff aware of the risk.
- Transfer the risk to a third party using insurance.
- Accept a risk where the entity believes the risk is low and that the downside is acceptable. For example, allowing senior dressage riders, if they so choose, to wear top hats rather than hard hats.

Management of risk, and in particular health and safety and safe-guarding children, should be discussed regularly by the board and further steps to reduce or mitigate risk be considered.

All serious incidents should immediately be recorded and reported through the proper channels in the organisation and brought to the attention of the board. Training is essential to ensure that board members are up to date on current thinking, for example about concussion, back protectors and prohibited substances.

Disclaimers are useful to make people aware of foreseeable risks of injury or their responsibility for possessions. Displaying a disclaimer or asking a person to sign a disclaimer does not completely absolve the entity from being held liable. However they are useful to make sure that people have been warned of the risks.

Communication is an excellent way of reducing risk. The board should be in touch with its members and stakeholders and listen to their concerns.

Accountability for Risk

Accountability for managing risk rests with the board. The board may create a risk committee (see Chapter 3: Committees) to deal with the area in greater detail. The board members should ensure that the committee should be adequately resourced with appropriate members and training if necessary. But the board members cannot delegate accountability to the risk committee. They must consider the reports of the risk committee and take the decisions themselves.

UNDERSTANDING THE ACCOUNTS

It is not a good sign if the accounts cannot be produced when requested or answers and reasonable explanations are not forthcoming. Each board member must be persistent and keep questioning until they understand the information they are being presented with. Each board member needs answers that they can understand, and/or the training to help them understand. The board member should not give in until they are confident that they are fulfilling their duty as a board member. This can be challenging, particularly when a board is made up of sports people who know the intricacies of the sport but are not that literate in reading figures.

Incorporated Entities

All board members of a company are equally responsible in law for financial controls and the reporting of financial performance. Anyone who acts as a board member is well advised to get training if they are not comfortable in dealing with the financials. It is important to note that in a company the accounts are not the responsibility of the treasurer or financial board member but of each and every member of the board.

Every year in their report to the members, of any incorporated sporting entity, the board must state that:

- They are responsible for preparing the financial statements and the board members' report
- They are satisfied that the financial statements give a true and fair view of the financial position and the income and expenses for the year

- They have selected suitable accounting policies
- They have made judgements and estimates that are reasonable
- They believe it is appropriate to prepare the financial statements on a going concern basis, i.e. to presume that the entity will continue

In addition, they acknowledge that they, i.e. each board member regardless of their knowledge of accounting, are responsible for keeping or causing to be kept adequate accounting records.[128] These records must be sufficient to:

- Record and explain the transactions of the company
- Enable the financial position of the company to be determined at any time
- Enable the financial statements to be prepared and audited

The records must be kept at the company's registered office or where the board members think fit.[129]

The board members are also responsible for safeguarding the assets of the company and taking reasonable steps for the prevention and detection of fraud and other irregularities.

When the financial statements are approved by the board and signed it is a serious offence if a board member knows that they do not give a true and fair view.[130] All board members are considered culpable unless it can be shown that they took all reasonable steps to prevent their approval.[131] Note it does not matter who actually signs the accounts, each board member is responsible.

With these heavy responsibilities every board member should ask for the accounts of the company to be produced at regular intervals during the year, e.g. quarterly, and they should be prepared to ask questions. They should be alert against poor explanations or late figures and insist on the figures at the earliest possible convenience.

Unincorporated Entities

In an unincorporated entity there is no reason why the standards should be lower. Arguably standards should be higher because of the risk of unlimited liability.

Management Accounts and Financial Statements[132]

An entity prepares management accounts for use by the board and other stakeholders such as lenders. Management accounts can be in any format. They show how the entity is performing. Performance may be measured against budget or against prior years. There may be key performance indicators (see Chapter 6: Measuring Success and Key Performance Indicators) that the board members have selected to assess the performance of the entity. These might include net increase in members, number of falls, liquidity ratios and so on.

Management accounts should be used to monitor income and expenditure against the budget on a regular basis, as well as cashflow and investments.

All companies are obliged to prepare statutory financial statements annually for their members, including an income and expense account and a balance sheet. The income and expense account shows revenue and expenses during the period, while the balance sheet shows the assets and liabilities of the entity at a particular date, e.g. 31 December. The financial statements must also include the accounting policies[133] which explain how certain items are shown in the financial statements. There must also be notes which give more detail,[134] for example an analysis of creditors.

All companies must include in their financial statements a directors' report which shows:[135]

- The names of the board members who served during the year
- The principal activities of the company

- A statement of the measures taken by the directors to secure compliance with keeping of accounting records and where they are kept
- Details of any important events after the financial year end
- A review of the business of the company
- A description of the principal risks and uncertainties
- A statement that there is no relevant audit information of which the auditors are unaware

The financial statements should be widely available and easy to access on the organisation's website.

SYSTEMS AND CONTROLS[136]

The board must ensure that appropriate systems and controls are in place. Good systems and controls give members, funders and sponsors comfort. Transparency brings a sporting entity credibility and allows it to gain trust. Effective controls ensure that limited funds are used in the most efficient manner.

Systems are how things work and, when written, are set out in the constitution or a series of policies. The policies and procedures should be communicated to board members, staff, volunteers or members as appropriate. The board approves all policies and should review them every couple of years. Polices are part of the overall control of the organisation.

The law insists on certain controls, e.g. the keeping of adequate accounting records, but other controls may come from funders, e.g. they might insist that the sporting entity complies with the Sports Code or that there are restrictions as to who can sign on behalf of the entity. They may also insist on the sporting entity accounting for the use of donations. At a minimum an entity should have written rules as to who can make payments, who is responsible for keeping the accounts and presenting them regularly to the board, and how resources, i.e. funds and people, are allocated.

Role of the Board in Implementing Controls

The board members of a sporting entity must not ignore controls. It is not their money that they are dealing with but that of the entity, that of their members and stakeholders. There is a possible risk that board members siphon off money, creating sub-funds or cash reserves, maybe cash in a box, for 'just in case ...', perhaps in genuine but misguided concern for the future of the entity. A particular danger area is where entities have a large number of bank accounts, not all of which are monitored regularly.

Board members should not be overly focused on the details of the playing of the sport; their role is in developing policies and control. They may see putting in controls as an expensive luxury, particularly if they do not have the knowledge internally and have to commission reports from auditors or consultants. Board members and volunteers may believe that there is no need for 'business controls' and may be offended at the lack of trust. For instance, there may be resistance to two signatories on the bank account or limits on spending. They may take the approach that they will deal with an issue when it arises, e.g. discrimination or lack of facilities for disabled members. This is, however, poor governance. It is much cheaper to prevent incidents than deal with them when they arise. The board must ensure that controls are in place and, where relevant, that the executive has implemented those controls.

Types of Controls

The concept of 'controls' is wide and may include:

- Performance measurement
  - strategic plan – budget
  - regular reporting of committees and the executive
- Expenditure controls
  - who has the authority to pay for expenses
  - what can be claimed for travel and subsistence
  - what expenditure can only be authorised by the board

- Accounting controls
  - reconciliation of debtor and creditor accounts, for instance, so that the amount the sport has in its books is the same as the debtor or creditor has in their books
  - method of banking receipts
  - reconciliation of the bank account with the accounting records
  - adequacy of reserve funds
  - ensuring that legal ownership of all assets is in the name of the entity[137]
  - restrictions on the use of cash
- Company secretarial for incorporated entities
  - ensuring that returns to the company register are made on time
  - ensuring that if the entity ceases to exist assets go to an appropriate organisation.
  - list of board memberships of all other companies by board members
  - beneficial ownership registration[138]
- Reporting
  - reports from committees, the treasurer, health and safety regularly made to the board
- Communication
  - explanation of policies to staff, members and volunteers

Of all controls one deserves special attention, and that is the segregation of duties. This is commonly disregarded and is often considered impractical. If observed, it is one of the strongest defences against fraud. The person responsible for making payments should not write up the books. Even in a small organisation these roles should be separated. This is not a matter of lack of trust, it is one of the most important controls in any organisation. Similarly, no one person should receive, record and deposit funds.

It is hard to prevent collusion, particularly when senior individuals are involved and a junior employee goes along with them, perhaps for fear of their job.

Too often it is said, 'Mrs X is the most dedicated, honest person I've ever met.' But the people who steal are the people who are trusted. If they were not trusted they wouldn't have the opportunity to steal. Individuals may steal with the initial intention of paying it back. It is difficult to know the stresses an individual may be under in their personal life – divorce, gambling, a sick child, their own health. When under pressure it is easier to convince themselves that they are just borrowing the funds.

It is the role of the board to ensure that adequate controls are in place. Board members should also never be seen to flout them.

ROLE OF THE EXTERNAL AUDITOR

The Companies Act requires companies over a certain size to have an audit of their financial statements. The audit is an independent examination of the financial statements that have been prepared by the board members. Its purpose is to give the members confidence in the accounts. The audited accounts may also be used by funding organisations and the Revenue Commissioners.

The auditors express their opinion as to whether the financial statements are prepared in all material respects in accordance with accounting standards and with company law, and whether the balance sheet and income and expense accounts are true and fair.

The auditors are not there to search for fraud and do not check every transaction. Auditors do sometimes catch fraudsters. Certainly, having an audit may deter a fraudster. But it is not a guarantee that there is no fraud.

There is nothing to stop an unincorporated entity from having an audit, apart from cost. In many organisations the constitution will require that an audit is carried out. Furthermore, if the company has income in excess of €250,000 it must have an audit to keep its Sports Body Tax Exemption (see Chapter 9: Tax).[139]

Audit Exemption

A company can apply for an exemption from audit if it is a small or micro company and has filed its annual return on time. If the board members take the decision to avail of the exemption, they then notify the members. The members can object and insist on an audit[140] and in the case of a company limited by guarantee any one member can object.[141]

Different rules as to the necessity of an audit apply if the entity is funded by Sport Ireland. Depending on the size of the grant, Sport Ireland may require an independent accountant's review and even a statement from the auditor that the grant was expended for the purpose intended by Sport Ireland. Any funded body may be subject to an audit by Sport Ireland auditors and if 50 per cent or more of its income is sourced from Exchequer funds then it may also need to make its books and records available to the Comptroller and Auditor General.

The decision for smaller entities as to whether to have an audit is difficult as an audit is relatively expensive. The cost of an audit may be deemed by the members as unreasonable and they would prefer to put all such funds into the sport. The board members must weigh up the benefits of an audit – added transparency, accountability, confidence in the figures and in the organisation itself – against the cost. An audit can also be of comfort to the board members, who have the responsibility of looking after the company's resources, and to donors or sponsors.

Another benefit of an audit for the board members is that the auditors prepare a letter to the management highlighting weaknesses in systems and controls that they noticed during the audit. This helps the board members focus their efforts on improving the effectiveness and efficiency of the company. The board should always ask for the management letter and consider it.

ROLE OF INTERNAL AUDITORS AND THE AUDIT COMMITTEE

Internal Audit

An internal audit differs from an external audit in that internal auditors report to the board while the external auditors report to the members. An internal auditor may be a separate committee or a working group within a sporting entity. In a smaller entity it can be an individual. External professionals can be hired to perform an internal audit review. There are specialist internal audit companies that will perform a specific audit. An internal audit helps board members to ensure compliance with the rules of the entity and be confident in the company's reports. It ensures that internal controls are being adhered to. Unlike external auditors, internal auditors may be specifically tasked with finding fraud or identifying opportunities for improvement in the running of the affairs of the entity. For instance, an internal audit might find unsupported expenses, unapproved credit card usage or unaccounted-for complimentary tickets.[142]

The board members or executive may resist internal audits. They may want to be in control, be fearful of the weaknesses that it may show or simply consider it a waste of time. It is a good sign of the health of an organisation if internal audits are properly resourced and supported by the board.

The Audit Committee

The audit committee is a board committee in that it reports directly to the board. The Sports Code recommends that the audit committee should have three or more board members as members, one of whom has recent and relevant financial experience. It may be useful to include non-board members with experience in finance or audit. The chair of the board may be a member of the audit committee but should not chair the audit committee. If the entity has independent non-executive board members, one or more should be on the audit committee.

The work of and attendance at audit committee meetings should be included in the annual report to members. Audit committees should not be regarded as a threat or staffed with people who 'will not rock the boat'. They are a strong governance tool for use by the board.

The audit committee monitors and reviews, and, if necessary, makes appropriate recommendations to the board on key financial issues.

The Accuracy of the Financial Statements of the Organisation

The financial statements, or accounts, are the collective responsibility of the whole board. It is the role of the audit committee to go through the financial statements in detail and ask questions of the treasurer, finance department or auditors to ensure that all members of the committee understand them. The audit committee is expected to report on the financial statements to the board.

Announcements about the Organisation's Financial Performance and Financial Controls

Financial control is vital to the integrity of a sporting entity. Any views expressed by the chair or the board on the entity's financial performance or controls should be cleared with the audit committee to ensure that such a remark is accurate and could not be construed as misleading.

Control and Risk Management Systems

The audit committee should insist that financial controls are in place, for instance that there are always two signatures for a payment. They should also ensure that risk is discussed regularly at board level.

The Effectiveness of the Organisation's Internal Audit Role

The audit committee should assess the work and resources available to internal auditors and report to the board accordingly. The audit committee should ensure that the board and the executive understand the purpose, authority and role of the internal audit function.

The External Auditor's Independence and the Effectiveness of the Audit Process

It is the role of the audit committee to ensure that external auditors are independent and that they are given the information to work effectively. The audit committee should approve the terms of engagement of the external auditor and their remuneration and put this recommendation to the annual general meeting.

Arrangements for Staff to Raise Concerns in Confidence about Possible Improprieties Relating to Financial Reporting or Other Matters

The entity should have a policy on 'whistleblowing' or good faith reporting. The audit committee is a suitable forum for such concerns to be raised. No person who, in good faith, reports a concern should be subject to retaliation or negative consequences, and reports of concerns and related investigations must be kept confidential as far as possible.

INSURANCE[143]

Insurance is used to reduce risk in a sport, and it is a fundamental part of risk management (see Chapter 7: Insurance). To minimise risk and protect against possible insurance claims every sporting entity should ensure that:

- They run their sport according to best practice and what is the norm for similar entities
- They take reasonable actions to avoid injury while acknowledging the particular risks of injury in that sport
- All equipment is in good working order
- Trainers, coaches and other professional staff regularly update their skills and are aware of updates in safety and safeguarding children
- There is good signage
- Participants follow relevant safety instructions

Types of Insurance Policy

Employers' Liability

This covers a sporting entity should an employee blame it for injury or property damage, for example concussion cases in professional sport.

Public Liability

This protects a club with respect to their legal liability to third parties for bodily injury or any loss or damage to material property which happens in connection with the activity of the club. This is a key insurance as no one can predict what accidents may occur. For example, a member may trip and fall on the premises.

Personal Accident

Personal accident cover insures against personal injury and gives a lump-sum benefit for accidents resulting in death or permanent disablement, physiotherapy, dental expenses, hospitalisation, and medical and rehabilitation expenses. Insurers can also provide a weekly benefit if a player is unable to work following an accident. This may cover all members playing in an entity. For instance, a player in a cricket club may be protected if hit on the head and permanently disabled. Some NGBs provide access to umbrella insurance policies while others insist their affiliates take out separate policies.

Professional Indemnity Insurance

This covers professional advice given by the sporting entity, including staff, coaches, child welfare officers, physiotherapists and nutritionists. For example, if an athlete has over-exercised, resulting in injuries, and the physiotherapist has failed to advise on correct parameters of exercise or has not shown the athlete how to use equipment correctly, the sporting entity may be liable for the bodily injury incurred.

Property Insurance

This protects physical property and equipment against loss from theft, fire or other risks. Buildings and their contents and money can be covered. This is important for sports with expensive portable equipment, for instance motorsports with cars, parts and tools.

Travel Insurance

Travel insurance may protect members, athletes and coaches when travelling abroad for competition or training. It may include medical expenses, cancellation, delayed baggage and travel delays.

Directors' and Officers' Insurance (D&O)

This protects board members and officers of the entity against claims made against them personally. D&O insurance protects board members and officers against claims arising out of wrongful acts and may cover breach of duty or trust, defamation, wrongful trading, neglect, error or misstatement. On the other hand, it does not usually cover fraud or dishonesty, pollution, pending litigation, or failure of computer systems.

Members v Non-Members

Members of a sporting entity voluntarily participate in a sport and accept the risks that are inherent in that sport. If they are registered, they participate at their own risk. There is no legal obligation for the entity to insure them, although they may choose to do so. The responsibility for cover rests with the individual member.

If a member is not paid up, they are simply a member of the public, and if they are injured while at the entity, they may sue the entity. It is therefore important that no unregistered members participate at an event, unless there are separate provisions with the insurance company for day members or guests to participate.

Prompt Notification

The sporting entity should notify their broker or insurance company promptly of any accident or incident as a claim may not be covered if notification is not made on time. The insurance company is interested in the risk. It is a false saving not telling the insurance company of problems as when a claim arises, they may not pay out.

Health and Safety Rules

Regardless of the level of insurance the board members should ensure that there are health and safety rules in place to keep the sporting entity safe for members and volunteers. These rules should be posted where visible to all and be available to members online. A sporting entity should carry out risk assessments at all events and offices to reduce risk. Checks such as checking the toilets, ensuring that glasses are not lying around and that all spillages are addressed should be documented.

Risks Associated with Not Incorporating

Many sporting entities are simply a collection of individuals. This has the advantage that costs are lower. There is no need to make returns to the Companies Registration Office. There may be no need for an audit. Meetings are not constrained by law but rather by the entity's rules or founding document. Members may appreciate this, believing that the focus is therefore kept on the sport.

Theoretically there is no reason why an unincorporated body might not enjoy some of the advantages of a company without the burden of the responsibilities under the Companies Act. If it wishes, it can organise an audit, have formal meetings, publicise its policies on the internet and be entirely transparent. There is no reason why it does not implement the Sports Code. Trustees can look after property, banks are happy to lend and sponsors to fund.

There are two reasons to incorporate. The first is to reduce risk. No one knows what disaster is looming. No one knows if a member is going to take offence and attack the club for defamation or under data protection rules. A startling example is that of Talbot and the Hermitage Golf Club, where a member sued the club for €10 million for damage to his reputation as a result of lowering his handicap. He lost the defamation case after 83 days in the High and Supreme Courts.[144]

The other reason is discipline and governance. In practice, having the rigour of the Companies Act forces better governance. Board members are legally bound by their fiduciary duties (see Chapter 2: Board Members' Duties).

If a club is not incorporated as a legal entity there is no limited liability for its members. It may be argued that the entity has insurance so why do they need limited liability? Those who have claimed under household or car insurance know that the proceeds of insurance rarely meet expectations and that there is likely to be an excess that must be borne by the claimant.

If an entity is incorporated, i.e. a company, it can sue and be sued in its own name. However, if it is not a company, it cannot bring or defend legal actions in its own name, i.e. as a club. Instead the claim or the defence must be by individual representative defendants who act on behalf of all the members at that time. It can become complicated when there are dissident members of the club suing the other members. The ability of the unincorporated club to bear the legal costs may also be open to question and members may be exposed.

Incorporation protects both the board members and the members of the club. However, entities may find the regulated environment which companies must comply with, such as CRO filings, burdensome and object to the expense of the administrative and legal work. Board members may fear the responsibilities of their legal duties.

As clubs become increasingly professional, commercialisation increases and the demand for strong governance grows, more and more clubs are moving to incorporate. However, there will always be local amateur clubs for whom the cost of incorporating is simply too high.

DISASTER RECOVERY/CONTINUITY PLANS[145]

When assessing risk, the board should consider disaster recovery and continuity plans. Disasters may include:

- A major injury or death
- An external incident such as a bomb/scare or pandemic
- Fire or theft of important assets
- Loss of data
- Cyber attack

The key is to focus on prevention. However, in preparation for a disaster the board should:

- Ensure there is a clear fire safety plan in place
- Ensure all officials have an emergency contact list

- Know who is responsible for informing the insurance company or broker
- Ensure backups of data are taken regularly and are tested to check that they can be reinstalled
- Know who takes command and what to do if the chain of command is broken
- Know who manages PR and keeps the members and the public informed
- Be aware of what authorities need to be informed, e.g. Data Protection Commissioners
- Ensure that first aid supplies are stocked, in date and easily accessible
- If there is a defibrillator check its power source

When there is incident ask:

- Has anyone been hurt?
- Is it safe to continue activities?
- Has everyone been moved to a safe place?
- Have photos been taken before anything is cleared?
- Have accident report forms been completed?
- Has everyone been contacted?
- What equipment/property is needed to get back in action?

It is essential that all stakeholders, funders, donors and members are kept informed. Recovery of systems, continuity plans and fire alarm procedures should be tested at regular intervals to minimise disruption in a crisis.

Carefully considered and tested disaster recovery procedures are invaluable when disaster strikes. These include communication between board members and media spokespeople. Having emergency procedures documented for every event can save lives.

THE SMALLER ENTITY

Risk Management and Controls

Every sporting entity should make sure that there are appropriate internal financial and management controls.[146] Segregation of duties where the person writing up the books is not responsible for signing cheques is an important control and every effort should be made to observe it.

Understanding the Accounts

A sporting entity should have a budget for income and expenditure and monitor this over the year.[147] This is particularly important if a key source of income, for instance sponsorship by a local business, fails to appear.

Insurance and Disaster Recovery

Insurance is important to mitigate risk. The entity should review all risks[148] and decide which ones they can manage.

Risk assessments should be routinely carried out before events. Contact numbers and procedures for emergencies should be available. Evacuation drills should be tested and disaster recovery plans discussed.

Other Areas

Particular attention must be paid to safeguarding children, doping and data protection. The club should discuss backup procedures with its IT manager.

CONCLUSION

An important function of any board is to understand and monitor risk and how to mitigate it, whether through insurance or controls. Audit, internal audit and audit committees are all useful tools to give a board comfort and reduce risk. Incorporation certainly limits liability and should be considered in all but the smallest entities.

Ten Key Points

1. The entity should do a risk assessment of the risks that it faces and then consider how to mitigate them.

2. The amount of risk that an entity and its members tolerate – their risk appetite – varies from entity to entity.

3. All board members are equally responsible in law for financial controls and the reporting of financial performance. The accounts are not the responsibility of the treasurer or financial board member but of each and every member of the board.

4. The management accounts show how the entity is performing. Performance may be measured against budget or against prior years. There may be key performance indicators that the board members have selected to assess the performance of the entity. These might include net increase in members, number of rider falls or liquidity ratios.

5. All companies are obliged to prepare statutory financial statements annually for their members, including an income and expense account and a balance sheet.

6. The purpose of an external audit is to give the members confidence in the accounts. An internal auditor helps board members to ensure compliance with the rules of the entity and be confident in the entity's reports.

7. Internal audit differs from external audit in that internal auditors report to the board while external auditors report to the members. Unlike external auditors, internal auditors may be specifically tasked with finding fraud or identifying opportunities for improvement in the running of the affairs of the entity.

8. Insurance is used to reduce risk and is a fundamental part of risk management.

9. Many sporting entities are unincorporated. This has the advantage that costs are lower. There are two key reasons to incorporate: to reduce risk and to improve discipline.

10. The board should ensure that recovery plans, continuity plans and fire alarm drills are tested. Communication lines in times of disaster or stress need to be considered. Carefully thought-out plans are invaluable should disaster occur.

ACCOUNTABILITY

- Introduction
- Accounting to Stakeholders
- General Meetings
- Expenses Policy
- Gifts and Donations
- Conflicts of Interest and Loyalty
- Board Members as Champions of the Organisation
- Board Confidentiality
- Being Ethical
- The Smaller Entity
- Conclusion
- Ten Key Points

INTRODUCTION

An entity must be transparent and accountable, communicating to its stakeholders. Transparency means letting stakeholders know what the organisation is doing. This breeds trust and confidence in the sporting entity.

Ethics starts at the top. Board members must be seen to support clear ethical policies, particularly on expenses, gifts, donations and conflicts of interests.

It is important to have a clear written code of ethics as people from different backgrounds and philosophies have different tolerances.

ACCOUNTING TO STAKEHOLDERS[149]

A stakeholder is someone who has a significant interest in the work of an entity and as such they want to be kept informed (see Chapter 6: Stakeholders and External Influencers). A stakeholder may be a member, a donor, the government, Sport Ireland, the media, or simply a debtor or creditor. If an entity is seen as accountable and transparent this helps to develop and maintain trust amongst stakeholders, particularly those responsible for the development of the sport.

The board should identify its key stakeholders and make sure that there is an agreed spokesperson who regularly liaises with them and makes available information to them on a regular basis. There should be a clear way for the stakeholders to communicate with the organisation and a process for the consideration of any complaints received from stakeholders. The board should ensure that complaints are adequately dealt with. Reputational issues, in particular, need to be monitored and decisive remedial action taken.

In sporting entities, member perceptions that the board is not listening to its members can gain currency very fast. The board must be seen to be listening and to take into account the opinions of members, even if they do not agree with them. It is crucial to engage with the members and to be seen to be doing so throughout the year and not only at the AGM.

Transparency

All stakeholders are interested in what goes on in the sport. The organisation's website is particularly useful for the publication of information. Board members who are athletes may be resistant to non-sport information being on the website; however funders and members want the sporting entity to be transparent and seen to be well-governed. Nevertheless, the importance of personal contact and meetings should not be underestimated. Information on the website might include:

- The strategy of the entity and progress against it
- The financial statements
- The structure of the organisation, the constitution and rules
- Terms of reference of the board and key committees
- Names and details of board members
- Identification of the chair and independent non-executive board members
- Remuneration (if any) of board members and senior management
- Policies, in particular health and safety, anti-doping and safeguarding children[150]
- Efforts to promote diversity and equality
- Results from engaging with elite athletes and other stakeholders
- Summarised minutes of the AGM and board meetings
- Governance statement, reflecting compliance with the Sports Code and any significant actions the board has taken or is taking, for instance reviewing strategy, changing its constitution, results of audit, and board member attendance at board meetings

Transparency is important. A good example is that the Olympic Federation of Ireland issues a summary of its key discussion and action points from its board meetings to all its membership. All codes and standards of practice to which the entity subscribes should be publicly stated and on the website.

Stakeholder Information[151]

All contact details should be kept in a safe place and should not be released to a third party without the person's consent. In accordance with GDPR only necessary personal information should be held.

Submitting Accounts to Members and Stakeholders

The AGM is when the accounts are presented to the members for consideration and members may choose to question the performance of the board. Making audited accounts available to other stakeholders allows trust in the organisation to be built. This is particularly important for funders, as well as members and creditors. The accounts should not be seen as a specialist area for the treasurer and the chair. They should be available to all stakeholders on the website.

Complying with the Sports Code

The Sports Code is there to help the board members run the organisation well. Compliance with the Sports Code reflects well on the entity. It shows that the entity is making every effort to run the entity in the best possible manner on behalf of its members and other stakeholders.

   If an entity is not compliant or is struggling to introduce the Sports Code, it reflects weaknesses in the administration. It may well be that while the sport has many excellent sportspeople on its board, it does not have sufficient leaders who know how to run an entity. A successful sport needs both.

GENERAL MEETINGS[152]

General meetings are meetings of all members. It is vital that an annual general meeting (AGM) and an extraordinary general meeting (EGM) follow the entity's constitution to the letter and, where the sporting entity is a company, the Companies Act 2014. Dissident members can be quick to protest if procedures were not followed correctly. If an error is made it is quite possible that the meeting is declared unconstitutional and the whole process, with the associated time and expense, must be started again.

The running of the general meetings should be planned carefully with regard to the workload and responsibility spread. If there is no legal or constitutional knowledge on the board, it is advisable to have the process and documents overseen by a lawyer.

Introducing change or surprising members at a general meeting can generate hostility. Important issues, for instance constitutional change, should be raised beforehand, preferably in informal forums. Members should be allowed to express their views. On the other hand, disaffected groups may try to avoid prior discussion and make a stand at the AGM. Board members should consider their response in advance of the meeting. The chair must ensure orderly conduct of the meeting while allowing members' opinions to be heard.

General meetings are an ideal forum for all members to come together. It is a great opportunity for members to feel part of a successful entity and to socialise. The business part of the meeting should not be allowed to overrun. Ideally there should be time at the end for members to relax.

Members may either attend the meeting or, if the constitution allows, vote by postal ballot or proxy, although most sporting entities require delegates to attend meetings. The disadvantage of only allowing those in attendance to vote can mean that those who live further away are not represented and the entity is led by a larger central region. For example, if meetings are generally held in Leinster this disadvantages the, perhaps very many, voters who live in the west, the south and the north. Proxy can overcome this difficulty. However, voting by proxy can slow down proceedings significantly and can be a considerable administrative burden.

General meetings should be carefully planned as they can be relatively easily hijacked by a discontented minority. It is advisable that the wording of all resolutions is checked with the legal advisor. The chair needs to keep control, allowing debate but controlled debate. If a discontented faction is expected it is advisable to have professional advisers at hand

Annual General Meetings[153]

The AGM of a company is run according to the Companies Act. It covers:

- Consideration of the financial statements, the board members' report and the auditor's report, if relevant
- Review by the members of the company's affairs
- Appointment of the auditors, if relevant
- Election and re-election of the board members
- Remuneration of the board members, if relevant

The members consider the financial statements but do not have to approve them. At the AGM they may ask questions about the accounts. The meeting should be well-chaired to ensure that the debate is orderly.

The members can use their power and not reappoint board members up for re-election, or, if allowed by the constitution, not approve the remuneration of the board members. They can also choose to change auditors. The AGM of an unincorporated entity will follow the rules set out in its constitution.

Extraordinary General Meetings

Any meeting of the members of a company other than an AGM, as described above, is an EGM. An EGM might be called to amend the constitution or to appoint a liquidator. An EGM can be called by the board members or if 10 per cent of voting members[154] ask the board members to call one. Constitutions of unincorporated entities usually allow for EGMs, whether they are described as such or not.

Notice of General Meetings

In a company 21 days' clear notice must be given for an annual general meeting and any extraordinary meeting where a special resolution is to be passed, or longer if that is what the constitution says. Any other general meeting, perhaps one to react to a major event, must have at least seven days' notice,[155] unless the constitution requires more; many companies limited by guarantee opt for fourteen days. Shorter notice can be given if agreed by all members (and if it is not inconsistent with the constitution) and the auditors.[156] It is vital that notice periods are strictly observed as inaccurate notice can invalidate a meeting.

The notice should state:

- The place, date and time
- The nature of the business
- Details of any special resolution(s)
- Details about the use of proxies[157]

If a shareholder is tabling a resolution to remove a board member[158] or the incumbent auditors[159] they must give the company extended notice of 28 days and the procedure set out in the Companies Act must be followed to the letter.

If a company's constitution permits, notice may be sent to the members by email.[160]

Unincorporated entities are likely to have similar rules in their constitution, but the exact wording should be checked.

Expenses Policy

An area that often comes under scrutiny by stakeholders is the expenses claimed by the board and the executive. Every sporting entity should have a written expenses policy. Different people have different tolerances and it should be clear to all what is acceptable to reclaim.

All expenses for purchases must be authorised in writing by a suitable authority before purchase or be in accordance with a written policy. This might be done by email or in the minutes of a meeting. Ideally a separate form should be developed so that all the appropriate information is input. This authorisation should be submitted with the claim for reimbursement.

The policy should set out when mileage can be claimed. Mileage might be permitted at civil service rates, which are relatively generous.[161] Mileage can be a considerable expense for an organisation and board members should consider when it can be claimed. Board members should be aware that if mileage is claimed for travelling from home to board meetings it may be seen by Revenue as remuneration. The workplace is considered the place of the board meeting and you cannot claim travelling to work as an expense for tax.

All expenses must be vouched, without exception. A policy should be adopted for the use of credit cards, signing off on such cards and their limits. Credit cards are liable to abuse, and it is essential that appropriate expenses policies and disciplinary procedures are in place. Where possible, the use of credit cards should be avoided. Unvouched allowances should not be tolerated, even for the chair or CEO. Clear rules should be set out as to what can be claimed, in particular in relation to hotel stays. Revenue gives useful and relatively generous subsistence rates for international stays. Entities should be aware that some expenses may be considered by Revenue as benefits in kind. It is therefore essential that a detailed expenses policy is enforced. It is important to distinguish between expenses and salary. A grounds person may require expenses or may be a part-time employee. The approach should be clear.

GIFTS AND DONATIONS

Giving

When a sporting entity is giving gifts, it must question if this in the interest of the sport. The entity should not be a vehicle to fund the favoured charity of one of the board members. This is not the purpose of the organisation. Ideally, all gifts or donations should be a matter reserved for the board. The purpose of and reason for the gift should be clear. It should not be possible to construe the gift as a bribe.

If money raised at a sporting event is to be shared between two entities, it should be clear to all participating what the split is.

The giving of tickets can be emotive and controversial. A sporting entity should ensure that there are clear rules as to how tickets and perks are dispensed.

Receiving

It is important that, as in giving so in receiving, no gift or donation can be interpreted as a bribe. A policy should be made on the receipt of gifts by board members and the executive and a maximum gift value, say €50, should be enforced. Gifts should not be hidden remuneration.

Similarly, the source of donations may be questioned. The receipt of sponsorship should be a matter reserved for the board. Not only is there the bribery question, there is also the danger of negative PR if there are questions as to the background of the donor.

CONFLICTS OF INTEREST AND LOYALTY[162]

It is worth the board having a discussion about conflicts. What constitutes a conflict can be a matter of opinion. For instance, if a person is a board member of a sporting entity and their child is one of that sport's elite athletes, how should this conflict be managed? Certainly, the board member may have a heightened knowledge of international competition and, Ireland being a small country, they might be one of only a handful in that sport with that knowledge. The situation should be discussed openly and the conflict registered and then documented as to how it is being managed.

The register of interests should be regularly updated and should be reviewed at least annually. Ideally, conflicts of interest should be published to members.

A common conflict is where a board member has a loyalty to the people who elected them to the board rather than to the sport as a whole. This is a very natural reaction and may be even more complicated when the person who elected or nominated them remains in a position of power and can influence the board member, e.g. by selecting what committees they might sit on or even what funds might be available for any entity that they are associated with.

A board member must tell the board if they believe they might have a conflict of interest or loyalty, and other board members should not hesitate also to raise the issue if they perceive a conflict. Guidelines as to how the conflict is managed should be in a written policy, e.g. should the person leave the room when the matter is being discussed? This is not essential in law but is widely seen as good practice and is recommended by the Sports Code unless the board decides otherwise. The person concerned must be told of the decision reached. If they have a heightened knowledge of a topic, perhaps they should give their opinion and then leave when the issue is being voted upon.

BOARD MEMBERS AS CHAMPIONS OF THE ORGANISATION[163]

An organisation is led by the board members. It is therefore important for those board members to give a clear example. Board members should not be seen as being in a position where they can flout the rules, rather they lead by example.

As a leader, the board member is there to inspire people and, in turn, the entity to success. This also means keeping board confidentiality and not bad-mouthing fellow board members, athletes or other stakeholders. Bleating about fellow board members does not earn respect for the individual or the entity.

BOARD CONFIDENTIALITY[164]

Whatever decision is made in the boardroom, even though it may not be the opinion of all board members, that is the decision of the board. Difficult, grey decisions will not get discussed if members of the board are not confident that their opinion, expressed in the boardroom, will not be leaked. Board members rely on board confidentiality. They will not state their concerns if they are aware that their position on the issue is subsequently going to be discussed in public. For example, if a board member is concerned that a coach is not adhering to health and safety issues they will hesitate to state their concern if they are aware that it will be related back to the individual involved.

If a member strongly disagrees with a decision, they should still not broadcast their individual opinion. Information should be released according to the agreed policy, ensuring that the entity speaks with one voice.

Breaching confidentiality is a breach of fiduciary duty (see Chapter 2: Board Members' Duties) and exposes the person who breached the duty to being sued by the company and removed from office. The duty of confidentiality means not disclosing company information. Directors cannot use a company's information for their own or anyone else's benefit unless expressly permitted by the constitution or a resolution in a general meeting of members. An express statutory provision on whistleblowing can override confidentiality but lofty claims by a sole director that disclosure is in the interests of 'transparency' most certainly do not override it.

It should be noted that the duty of confidentiality continues when a director resigns or leaves a board.

BEING ETHICAL[165]

Ethics must start at the top of an organisation. The question has been debated for many centuries as to whether ethics can be taught. Ethics are a product of our upbringing, religious and philosophical beliefs, and culture. In any entity there may be a wide variety of ethical positions. One person might strongly believe that the death penalty is unethical, but others may believe that it is an appropriate moral solution. Or in a sporting context is it ethical to kneel during the American anthem in protest against racial inequality?

In any entity there needs to be guidelines; for instance, if it is acceptable or appropriate for an official or board member of a sporting entity to accept from a member, sponsor or supplier:

- A gift
- Lunch/dinner
- Hospitality at a local match or event
- Hospitality at an international match or event

Similarly, what is acceptable in terms of a sporting entity sending administrative or board members to a major international competition or the Olympic Games? Are they really needed? What is their role? Would the money have been better spent funding the athletes? Putting a clear travel and expenses policy in place is recommended to ensure these questions are answered.

Whether something is acceptable is not so much a question of right or wrong but what are the particular entity's values, or ethics? As ethics vary so much from person to person they need to be written down.

An ethics policy might cover:

- Gifts/hospitality
    - Giving gifts or perks to members or staff
    - Receiving gifts from customers
    - Attending conferences and/or outings funded by a supplier
    - Attending international sporting events
- Employee matters
    - Paying bribes
    - Bullying or harassment
    - Not protecting a whistleblower
    - Asking an employee to do something questionable
    - Exploiting vulnerable staff
- Financial reporting
    - Creative accounting
    - Misleading auditors
    - Being 'economical with the truth'
- Tax
    - Cash payments to officials and players
    - Use of offshore or special-purpose vehicles
- Safety
    - Illegal/irresponsible disposal of waste
    - Overweight vehicles
    - Disregarding safety equipment
    - Poor maintenance of property or equipment
- IT
    - Unlicensed software
    - Poor data protection
- Insolvency
    - Warning or tipping off favoured suppliers or customers not to supply goods as they may not get paid
    - Paying off only certain creditors
- Gambling/betting

- Who is barred from such activities?
- How is insider information handled?

The larger and more diverse the sporting entity, the more difficult it is to maintain consistency in the application of values and ethical behaviour. A well-written code, consistently applied, minimises uncertainty and raises awareness of ethical issues in the sport. Ultimately, good ethical practice in a sport should improve transparency and reduce the likelihood of reputational damage.

The responsibility of leading the board, and thus the sporting entity, in developing an ethical culture rests with the chair. The ethics policy may be a separate policy or incorporated into a written code of conduct. This must highlight the standards of behaviour expected and what happens if they are not met. Ethical standards do evolve, and the policy should be reviewed every two to three years to ensure it meets the standards of the stakeholders. All board members, on appointment, should sign a statement to indicate that they have understood the ethics policy. It must be applied equally to all individuals.

THE SMALLER ENTITY

Accounting to Stakeholders

The board should identify the stakeholders of the entity and make sure there is regular and effective communication with them.[166] The board should decide what stakeholders they need to communicate with, how often and who will be the agreed spokesperson.[167] There should be an annual meeting of members.

If a company, the members consider, rather than approve, the company's statutory financial statements and the report of the directors and, unless the company is entitled to and has availed of the audit exemption, the report of the auditors.

The annual meeting should be used to report on the activities of the year, listen to people's views about the work of the organisation and ensure that there is a clear system in place for dealing with correspondence, feedback and complaints to the organisation.[168] The meeting should also be used to consult with stakeholders if the board is planning to make significant changes to the way that the entity is run.[169] The annual activity report should be widely available on the entity's website or Facebook page.

Conflicts of Interest and Loyalty

The board should discuss conflicts of interest and conflicts of loyalty and decide how to address these.[170] Each board member and anyone else present must tell the board if they believe they have a conflict of interest on a matter to be decided on at a meeting. Unless the board decides otherwise, they must leave the room when the board is discussing or deciding on that matter. The person concerned should be told what decision was reached. Conflicts of interest must be recorded in the minutes.[171]

Reputation

All board members must understand their responsibility to act as champions for the group by promoting its work and reputation.[172]

Board members must be honest, fair and independent. The chair leads the board in developing an ethical culture in line with the values of the organisation.[173] A code of conduct sets the ground rules for board or committee members.[174] The code of conduct gives clear guidelines on the receipt of gifts or hospitality by board members.[175] An expenses and gifts policy is just as important in a small entity as a large one. All board members should sign a commitment to the code of conduct[176] and the code should be reviewed at least every three years.[177] Finally, the board members must be fair by consistently applying the same ethical standards to every person and situation.[178]

Confidentiality

Board members should maintain the confidentiality of board meetings to allow issues to be discussed openly. This should be set out in a code of conduct.[179]

CONCLUSION

Accountability is essential. The board needs to ensure that a robust culture of 'holding to account' operates and is seen to operate within the organisation. Constructive challenge is to be encouraged.

The reputation of an entity depends on its leadership. The chair and the board should lead by example. The board needs open challenge at the board table so that issues can be debated in full. Board members need to be able to speak in the boardroom confident in the confidentiality of such discussions.

Ten Key Points

1.   A stakeholder is someone who has a significant interest in the work of an entity and as such they want to be kept informed. If an entity is seen as accountable and transparent this helps to develop and maintain trust amongst stakeholders, particularly those responsible for the development of the sport.

2.   A general meeting is a meeting of the members. If there is no legal or constitutional knowledge on the board it is advisable to have the process and documents overseen by a lawyer. The AGM and notice thereof must be held strictly in line with the constitution and, where relevant, company law.

3.   The AGM is when the accounts are presented to the members for consideration and members may choose to question the performance of the board.

4. Every entity should have a written expenses policy. Different people have different tolerances and it should be clear to all what is acceptable to reclaim.

5. Ideally the giving and receiving of all gifts, perks or donations should be a matter reserved for the board. The purpose of and reason for the gift should be clear. It should not be possible to construe the gift as a bribe.

6. A board member must tell the board if they believe they might have a conflict of interest or loyalty and other board members should not hesitate also to raise the issue if they perceive a conflict. Guidelines as to how the conflict is managed should be in a written policy. All conflicts should be registered.

7. Board members should act as champions of the organisation. They are there to inspire people and, in turn, the sporting entity to success. Their behaviour must be seen to be ethical at all times.

8. A good reputation takes a long time to build up but is very easy to destroy.

9. The larger the entity, the more difficult it is to maintain consistency in the application of values and ethical behaviour. A well-written code of conduct, consistently applied, minimises uncertainty and raises awareness of ethical issues in the entity.

10. All board members, on appointment, should sign the code of conduct and ethics policy. It must be applied equally to all individuals.

9

Monitoring

- Introduction
- The CEO – Role and Responsibilities
- People Issues
- Safeguarding Children and Young People
- Company Law
- Tax
- Financial Obligations
- Integrity of Sport
- The Smaller Entity
- Conclusion
- Ten Key Points

INTRODUCTION

One of the most important people in a sporting entity is the CEO. The CEO may be a board member or attend board meetings on invitation. In a smaller entity the CEO may also act as chair. However, in larger organisations these roles should be split, with the CEO running the sporting entity and reporting to the board, and in person to the chair. The relationship between the CEO and the chair can be complex as the CEO is running the organisation under instruction from the board, which in turn monitors the CEO's performance.

The board is there not only to monitor the work of the CEO and the management team, but also to ensure compliance with the law and to safeguard the integrity of the sport.

THE CEO – ROLE AND RESPONSIBILITIES[180]

The CEO runs the sporting entity day-to-day and is responsible for leading management. They ensure that the decisions of the board are communicated to the management team and they report back to the board on the implementation of their decisions. In sporting, as in other organisations, there is a danger that the CEO may ignore the authority of the board or become overly dominant. It is vital that the CEO reports in full to the board and does not work to subvert or reinterpret decisions of the board or take decisions beyond the authority invested in them by the board.

The CEO's role is to manage the entity while the chair's role is to lead and manage the board. Neither the chair, nor any other board member, should encroach on the work of the CEO. The powers vested in the CEO may differ from entity to entity and may also depend on the skills and experience of the individuals. To avoid conflict, the division of responsibilities between the chair, the board and the CEO should be set out in writing in terms of reference that are reviewed by the board at regular intervals, e.g. every two years.

The CEO should report to the board not only on current operations but also on the requirements of regulators and funders, for instance the CRO, the NGB and sponsors. The CEO should have a clear job description which outlines when and who they report to on the board. Each year objectives should be set by the board for the CEO which are measurable and clearly identify the performance expectations of the CEO and which are in line with the strategic plan and the operational plans.

The constitution or terms of reference should set out whether the CEO should be a director. In non-profit organisations such as sporting entities it is vital that the board actively monitor the running of the entity and in particular the performance of the CEO. A strong CEO needs a strong board. On the other hand, the board needs to understand the complexities of running the business and the CEO's input is vital on strategy, risk and accountability. It should be noted that if things go wrong the CEO is often called to account as well as the board, who are legally responsible. A useful solution can be for the CEO not to be on the board but to be invited to the majority of meetings.

PEOPLE ISSUES[181]

One of the key roles of the CEO is managing employees and reporting to the board on any significant issues. This is a complex area and is likely to be one of the entity's largest costs as well as being an area of high risk. Specialist advice is essential to ensure that all legal obligations are complied with.

Employment Issues

Employee v Consultant

It can be tempting for an organisation to hire a person to work for them as a consultant rather than as an employee. When a person is a consultant and not an employee, then no PAYE and PRSI is paid by the entity and the employee has no employment rights. But Revenue has strict rules on the difference between an employee and a consultant. If the person has set hours, supplies labour only and cannot sub-contract the work they are likely to be an employee. A consultant may have several clients, be able to sub-contract work, own their own business, supply the tools of trade, e.g. computer, and bear financial risk.[182] Board members should be aware of the terms of all consultancy contracts and if they have any doubt as to whether the person should really be an employee, they should take advice.

Employee Contract and Employment Policies[183]

Every employee, on joining an entity, should be given a contract within two months. There are set requirements as to what should be covered in the contract.[184] They should have an up-to-date job description and receive a handbook of the policies of the entity, including the disciplinary and grievance procedures, whistleblowing procedures and code of conduct. It is convenient if the policies are kept on the website, easily accessible for the employees and visible to stakeholders.

Working Time

Employee working time and holidays can be a complex area[185] and if there are queries appropriate advice should be sought. It is important that issues such as payment for bank holidays for part-time workers and how many days' holiday part-time workers receive are ironed out early so both the employer and employee do not have unrealistic expectations.

Senior Staff Contracts

Senior employees are expensive for any sport. All senior employee contracts should be subject to a clear procedure and their approval a matter reserved for the board's decision. The whole board, rather than selected individuals, should manage the level of remuneration (including pensions, bonuses and any perks) paid to CEOs, high-performance managers and senior management. The whole board should be aware of delayed compensation, e.g. bonuses to be paid after a number of years, or golden parachute clauses where certain significant benefits are paid if employment is terminated.

In the role of monitor the board must ensure that appropriate policies are in place and that it has procedures where it can monitor compliance with these policies, e.g. by using internal audit. A remuneration policy in line with budget should be agreed by the board and if a remuneration/HR committee exists they should abide by that policy. Financial statements should at least set out the full amount spent on remuneration.

It should be noted that if a company is incorporated, the Companies Act[186] requires that board members must disclose their aggregate remuneration, including salaries, benefit-in-kind, fees and pensions. This is in addition to the disclosure of gross amounts paid to employees and numbers of employees, which are separately required.

The board should consider how the reputation of the sport and its administration would be affected should senior management remuneration become public and whether it will affect fundraising. Funders are willing to sponsor elite athletes and disadvantaged groups; they are less inclined to support a sport where there are high administrative salaries.

Dismissal or Redundancy

If the CEO recommends that an employee be dismissed or made redundant, specialist advice must be sought. If the board has concerns about the CEO this too needs to be managed and expert advice sought. This is an area that can be extremely costly if mishandled. There must be substantive grounds to justify the termination of a contract of employment, and fair procedures must be followed when effecting the termination of employment.[187]

Dismissal is likely to be judged unfair if it results from:

- Legal proceedings against an employer where they are a party or a witness
- Race, colour, sexual orientation, age or membership of the Traveller community
- Pregnancy, giving birth or breastfeeding, or any matters connected with pregnancy or birth
- Availing of rights under legislation to maternity leave, adoptive leave, paternity leave, carer's leave, parental leave or force majeure leave
- Unfair selection for redundancy
- Making a protected disclosure, i.e. whistleblowing (that is, where they raise concerns about possible wrongdoing at work) under the Protected Disclosures Act 2014
- Membership or proposed membership of a trade union
- Religious or political opinions

Extremely rancorous disputes can result with charges of defamation on one side and of gross misconduct on the other. Even if the dispute is settled the disruption and bad feeling cannot be underestimated. Similarly, if there is a reorganisation and it is the intention to make an employee redundant the CEO must ensure, and the board monitor, that correct procedures are followed. Redundancy is when the dismissal does not relate to the employee but to the requirements of the entity, for instance where the requirements of the sport for an employee to carry out work of a particular kind in the place where they were so employed have ceased.[188]

Employment costs are usually one of the highest expenses and therefore need to be actively managed. Employment-related claims, such as claims of bullying or harassment, can take up a huge amount of management time and be very stressful for all parties concerned. The board members must ensure that they provide staff with a safe place to work and ensure that the executive reports to them accordingly.

Procedure in employment-related issues is important. For instance, in a 2018 case the Workplace Relations Commission 'found that a gym "showed little regard to the principles of fair procedures and natural justice", noting that the complainant's bullying case was investigated by the person he was accusing and that he was not interviewed as part of it.'[189]

Athlete Welfare

A sporting entity has a responsibility for the welfare of its athletes. Whether this is making sure that their voice is heard, or investigating safety concerns in the sport, or simply promoting their physical and mental well-being. This may also involve assisting athletes in combining their sporting activities with education or work experience.

For instance, the Olympic Federation of Ireland has an athlete commission which covers:

- Athlete welfare – empowering athletes and stakeholders to develop welfare and education initiatives for athletes
- Games operations with input into OFI Olympic Games planning
- Awareness and communications ensuring visibility and transparency within the Irish Olympic movement

Volunteers[190]

The CEO is responsible for managing volunteers and their interaction with employees. This can be a difficult area. Volunteers are giving their time for free and as a result may not like being held accountable. A volunteer who accepts tasks and then does not complete them is a liability.

It should be noted that this also applies to unpaid board members. If an unpaid board member does not have the time to perform their role the entity will generally be better off without them. A volunteer policy should be adopted by the board to set out the roles of all volunteers.

The key to successful management of volunteers is to ensure that there is a policy for the recruitment, induction, support and supervision of volunteers. This involves training, either formal or informal. The more effort the entity invests in its volunteers the better their accountability is likely to be. The National Sports Policy aims to 'to sustain and grow our volunteer base.'[191] It sees this as an important area for investment, envisaging:

'... an annual volunteer training budget to be jointly administered by the NGBs and the LSP network to ensure that volunteer training can occur across sports. This training will focus on issues such as child welfare, disability awareness, first aid, sports administration and governance, and fundraising. The NGBs and LSPs will be expected to work closely with clubs and Sport Ireland Coaching in planning and delivering this training.'[192]

While volunteers need to be held accountable, they must also be thanked. People volunteer in sport for different reasons: a love of watching or being involved with the sport, a chance to meet and make friends, or an opportunity to give something back to the community. By creating a culture of volunteering and investing in volunteers, a strong sense of belonging between the entity, its members and volunteers develops, bringing success and social benefits.

It is important that health and safety rules and staff welfare rules are also applied to volunteers. The board must ensure that they operate in a safe environment. An example of where this failed is when in 2018 a volunteer referee was hospitalised as a result of an assault at a soccer match in the Midlands.[193]

The board must monitor volunteer policies and take steps to ensure that volunteers feel that they are appreciated and part of the club at the same time as being managed to ensure that they are effective.

Training

Board members, employees and volunteers should all be encouraged to upskill. The CEO should identify appropriate courses, such as health and safety, crowd control and safeguarding children. Board members should be included on such courses and would be expected to keep their relevant skills up to date.

The board members and the executive should be trained in governance. Sport Ireland recognises the importance of governance and, to assist sporting entities in adopting the Sports Code, it is to 'put in place the training and supports needed by different organisations to assist with the adoption process'.[194]

In addition, Sport Ireland is developing 'a long-term strategy for education, learning and development'. This addresses '... increased professionalisation, development, validation and recognition, provision for continuous professional development (CPD), diversity of leadership'.[195] The Sport Ireland Organisational Development and Change Unit is active in building the governance capability in the sports sector for entities that it funds.

As regulations change – for instance GDPR or safeguarding children – the board members and executive need to ensure that they, the employees and volunteers are aware of and being trained in the changes. Many volunteers appreciate training, and this encourages them to work more closely and effectively with the entity. A key area of training for all staff and volunteers is health and safety, and, for those running events, risk assessment.

The National Sports Policy aims 'to develop an education or information campaign to help parents/guardians to engage with their children to develop physical literacy and positive habits around sport and physical activity as part of an overall healthier lifestyle'[196] and for training to 'focus on issues such as child welfare, disability awareness, first aid, sports administration and governance, and fundraising'.[197]

Training should be considered in all sporting entities. Smaller entities may have a professional accountant, lawyer, or media person on the board who would be willing to give training or explain certain issues to the rest of the board, e.g. fiduciary duties. NGBs may also organise low-cost training for their affiliated entities.

Equality

The CEO must ensure and the board monitor that there is no discrimination against any individual or group. Employment law[198] prohibits discrimination across nine grounds:

- Gender
- Civil status
- Family status
- Age
- Race
- Religion
- Disability
- Sexual orientation
- Membership of the Traveller community

The policy on equality should not only cover employees but also consider volunteers and members. A sport should aim to remove the barriers faced by individuals who would like to be involved in sport, allowing disadvantaged groups to participate. The board should monitor equal opportunity and equal treatment in all policies and initiatives, and include equality and diversity in its strategy.

Diversification is important. Ideally the entity should promote on its website the efforts it is taking to ensure diversity and set clear diversity targets. Board members should insist on diversification in all senses of the word and ensure that there is a reasonable presence of independent voices to allow open debate, enabling better decision-making. Sport Ireland actively 'funds … and works with a range of organisations providing and promoting opportunities for people with disabilities to take part in sport and physical activity.'[199]

Some sporting entities may be concerned over their capacity and capability to include people with disabilities in their programme. The National Sports Policy aims to address this and in its principles for supports states 'delivering a sporting environment that can be accessed, understood and used to the greatest extent possible by all people regardless of their age, ability or disability will be prioritised.'[200] It sets an action to address participation by those with a disability: 'We will explore the possibility of introducing a national network of Sports Inclusion Disability Officers (SIDOs) aligned to the LSP network. These SIDOs would be expected to work closely with relevant NGBs, the disability sector, leisure centre providers, the CARA Centre and other stakeholders in providing opportunities for people with disabilities to take part in sport.'[201]

There has been huge progress in increasing the involvement of women in sport. Sport Ireland in 2019 launched its Women in Sport Policy, which recognises 'the opportunity to make a significant impact on the lives of women through their involvement in sport. Coaching & Officiating, Active Participation, Leadership & Governance, and Visibility are the four key target areas'.[202]

Another initiative, 20x20, has focused on media coverage and participation with the motto, 'If she can't see it, she can't be it'.[203]

Women in sport have become increasingly vocal, for instance the case taken by Eva Carneiro, a former Chelsea team doctor, against manager José Mourinho for sex discrimination and harassment.[204] Board members of sporting entities need to ensure that there are policies in place to ensure equality and no discrimination.

Racism in sport needs strong policing. A notorious example is Joe Marler, the Harlequins rugby player, who received a two-game ban and fine for calling Welsh player Samson Lee a 'Gypsy boy'.[205]

Similarly, the board must be alert to discrimination against disability. For instance, Jonás Gutiérrez, a footballer, won a disability discrimination claim against Newcastle United Football Club after he successfully argued that the club discriminated against him because of his disability, testicular cancer.[206]

Discrimination can also be on the grounds of age. Tennis Ireland was fined in 2017 for discrimination on grounds of age when it appointed its CEO over another candidate.[207]

SAFEGUARDING CHILDREN AND YOUNG PEOPLE

Safeguarding, a term that refers to the welfare and protection of young people and children, is a priority for all sports, even in the very smallest sporting entity. A child is considered to be an unmarried person under eighteen years of age.

Safeguarding Guidance for Children and Young People in Sport

Sport Ireland's *Safeguarding Guidance for Children and Young People in Sport* (2019)[208] is underpinned by Ireland's *Children First: National Guidance for the Protection and Welfare of Children* (2017)[209] and by *Co-operating to Safeguard Children and Young People in Northern Ireland* (2017),[210] as well as the requisite pieces of legislation. It was developed by Sport Ireland and Sport NI and provides templates and information for sporting entities to use to formulate their own safeguarding policies.

The guidance document has its foundation in the United Nations Convention on the Rights of the Child by recognising the core principles of integrity, fair play and providing a safe, enjoyable and inclusive environment in which children can learn and thrive in sport. The document sets out the requirements for recruiting and working with children and young people, as well as providing guidance on specific considerations for involving young people, e.g. behaviour of leaders, taking photographs, physical contact, communications, travelling and staying on away trips.

Every sporting entity should adopt the *Safeguarding Guidance*. Potential board members should be familiar with it and any specific safeguarding policies developed for their individual sporting entity. The board should ensure the requirements and policies are being implemented throughout the sporting entity.

Children's Officers (CO)

Safeguarding Guidance requires NGBs to appoint a national children's officer. The national children's officer should be a member of the board or have access to the board to ensure that children's interests are kept on the agenda, and that the children's officer can influence decisions of the board. The NGB policies should provide for the appointment of children's officers at each level of operation and in all affiliates, especially in their clubs.

    The role of the club children's officer, as stated in the *Safeguarding Guidance*, is:

> 'The appointment of Club Children's Officers in sports clubs/organisations is an essential element in the creation of a quality atmosphere. They act as a resource with regard to children's issues. In summary Children's Officers should review current policies in relation to young people, check that all activities are safe and fun, and inform adults of how to deal with any concerns that may arise in relation to the protection of children and young people. Club Children's Officers should be child centred in focus and have as the primary aim the establishment of a child centred ethos within the club. S/he is the link between the children and the adults in the club. S/he also takes responsibility for monitoring and reporting to the Club Management Committee on how club policy impacts on young people and Sports Leaders.'[211]

Designated Liaison Person (DLP)

The NGB must appoint a Designated Liaison Person, and again this appointment must cascade down to each level of the NGB. The DLP may or may not be the children's officer. The role of the DLP is to ensure the required reporting procedures are followed and to report any suspected cases of child neglect or abuse to the duty social worker in the Child and Family Agency/Tusla or an Garda Síochána/Gateway team or the PSNI.

Reporting

Children's officers/Designated Liaison Persons do not have the role of investigating a concern of harm to a child. Investigation of concerns of harm to a child or young person is the responsibility of the statutory authorities. Sporting entities, however, should have a policy and rules in place to take action to protect young people from risk of harm where an individual is reported to the statutory authorities following a safeguarding concern, disclosure or allegation. The policy should include dealing with the possible suspension of members/individuals and how to carry out a risk assessment following a statutory authority inquiry.

The CO/DLP can also take an informal consultation with duty social workers to discuss a concern to assess if it meets the threshold for reporting as a concern of harm to the statutory authorities.

Safeguarding Training

There are three levels of training courses available for sport leaders. Everyone involved with children and young people in sport must attend the basic level safeguarding course – Safeguarding Level 1. For anyone not directly in a role with children Safeguarding Level 1 is a recommendation, and this should apply to board members.

Children's officers must also attend the Safeguarding Level 2 – Club Children's Officer training and the appointed Designated Liaison Person must attend Safeguarding Level 3 – DLP. These are the training requirements as recommended by Sport Ireland in line with training stipulated in the Children First Act 2015.

All of these courses are available throughout the country and often directly from an NGB.

Vetting

In Ireland there are specific roles for which National Vetting Bureau (NVB) vetting is a legal requirement according to legislation. In

Northern Ireland it is a legal requirement not to recruit someone who is barred from working with children in a regulated activity position. Such a position is where there is unsupervised work with children once a week or more. Each sporting entity must identify the roles, according to the requirements of the legislation, that are required to have a valid vetting disclosure, or check before filling a position whether it requires a vetting disclosure or check. Generally, anyone who is involved in supervision, education or training of children is required to be vetted.

In Ireland vetting is carried out through a relevant organisation with an appointed liaison registered with the NVB. In Northern Ireland vetting is carried through a registered body with an appointed registered signatory registered with Access NI.

Most NGBs are registered with NVB and/or Access NI, and for those that are not there are some relevant organisations/registered bodies that can provide a vetting service.

Safeguarding Must Be on the Agenda

Safeguarding must be a top agenda item for sporting boards. Cases continue to come to light. For instance, in the UK an FA review was set up after former Crewe defender Andy Woodward spoke out about the alleged abuse he suffered from a coach.

In November 2018 James Torbett, a football coach at Celtic Boys' Club in Scotland, was jailed for six years after being convicted of abusing three boys over eight years in the 1980s and 1990s. Detective Chief Inspector Sarah Taylor, of the National Child Abuse Investigation Unit, said:

'Torbett was a predator who used football to allow him access to young boys .... He preyed on these boys, he exploited their dreams and he subjected them to callous and depraved abuse .... I have no doubt that he exerted control over the boys in his care and coerced them with promises and lies.'[212]

The US Safe Sport Policy has been overhauled to better police itself in the wake of the sexual abuse scandal surrounding Larry Nassar. The long-time doctor at both USA Gymnastics and Michigan State University is serving an effective life prison for possession of child abuse images and molesting young women – many of them female gymnasts – and girls under the guise of medical treatment.[213]

COMPANY LAW[214]

In addition to the importance of legalities when dealing with people, company law is an important consideration for the board to monitor. If an entity is a company the CEO must also implement company law and it is the duty of the board to ensure that this is done.

Companies Act

All sporting entities that are companies, rather than unincorporated entities, must be compliant with the Companies Act 2014.

The Companies Act 2014 is a lengthy piece of legislation, but it is clearly laid out. The first fifteen parts deal with the simple limited company. Most sporting entities are companies limited by guarantee (Clg), which are dealt with in Part 18. The rules of the limited company apply, i.e. Parts 1–15 unless the part on Clgs amends it. Although legal interpretation will usually be necessary, a board member should not hesitate to look up a section. The Act is on the internet and is easily searchable.[215] The Act is clear on the consequences of not complying with company law in each area. It lists four categories of offence, with punishments ranging from a €5,000 fine to a €500,000 fine and up to ten years' imprisonment.

The most serious offences, Category 1 and Category 2 offences, are primarily linked to insolvency and failure to keep accounting records. Board members should not underestimate the importance of keeping up-to-date accounting. For instance, inadequate accounting records for a company that is subsequently wound up and unable to pay its debts[216] is a Category 1 offence and the board members may be held personally liable.

The board should also monitor that the company secretary regularly reports to the board that all returns have been filed on time with the Companies Registration Office. It is the job of the CEO to ensure that this process is functioning.

Importantly, the Act lists the duties of a board member. If a board member reads only one section of the Act, they should look at the section on fiduciary duties, section 228 (see Chapter 2: Board Members' Duties).

TAX

Sports Body Tax Exemption

Sporting entities pay tax, whether they are a company or not, contrary to popular belief. There is a specific exemption for corporation tax, the Sports Body Tax Exemption, but this must be applied for and conditions met. Entities can register as a tax-exempt sporting body if they meet the required conditions:

> '[The Sports Body Tax Exemption can be granted] to a sports body whose sole purpose is to promote an athletic or amateur game or sport. Any income received by the sporting body must also be used for the purpose of promoting the game or sport.'[217]

The requirements for the tax exemption differ from company law. For instance, in company law a company can have a minimum of two board members but to benefit from the tax exemption there must be three. Similarly, accounts must be audited if turnover is in excess of €250,000.

There are certain paragraphs that Revenue insist are included in the constitution to avail of the exemption. Importantly, to avail of the exemption board members must not be paid, and no share of profits go to the members. On winding up the profits must go to another similar organisation. If the constitution is amended at all, it must be resubmitted to Revenue. This can delay the implementation of an amended constitution.

Companies such as golf clubs that make profits are treated as businesses rather than sporting clubs.

Tax Relief on Donations[218]

Tax relief on donations to a sports body is allowable if it is:

- To an approved sports body, and
- For an approved project

An approved sports body is one that is availing of the Sports Body Tax Exemption (see above). An approved project is one that is approved by the Department of Transport, Tourism and Sport. It should note that all projects are capital in nature, e.g. building a hard pitch, and not operational, e.g. supporting athletes going to an international competition.

The donation must be at least €250. Before giving such a donation the donor should check with the sporting entity and his tax accountant to ensure that the claim is eligible and made in the correct format.

PAYE

If an entity has employees, it must pay income tax under the PAYE system. Payments to referees, coaches and judges are not exempt. They may, however, be paid expenses and mileage expenses in line with civil service rates, which are relatively generous.[219]

FINANCIAL OBLIGATIONS[220]

Grants

An enormous amount of work may be put in by the executive to receive a grant. However, winning a grant is only the start.

The board must monitor, at regular intervals, how the executive uses the grant and if that use is strictly in accordance with the conditions of the grant. If an entity is no longer able to comply with a condition, e.g. that the money be invested in health and safety equipment which must be received before a certain date, they should discuss it with the grant giver. Transparency and honesty are key. Grants cannot, usually, be used retrospectively. The board should ensure that there is a clearly designated person responsible for the use of the grant and that the CEO reports on its use to the board.

The conditions pertaining to private donor grants must also be strictly observed. A private donor may give the funds for, say, video equipment. But if the entity only spends a portion of the grant on video equipment and the remainder on, say, wages the sponsor is within their rights to insist that the money is properly spent or repaid. It is unlikely that they will donate again.

The monitoring should involve liaison with the grant giver, accounting for the grant and acknowledgement once the grant process is complete.

Borrowing

Both short-term and long-term loans come with conditions. The conditions of an overdraft may be relatively straightforward as the overdraft is repayable on demand. There may be considerable conditions and warranties relating to a long-term loan. The board members should be aware of the terms of a loan and ask the CEO to report on compliance. If the entity is in any financial difficulty this is an area that the board must review very regularly.

Provision of Loans

While there is nothing inherently wrong with accepting a loan from an individual, sporting entities must do their due diligence. Is the board in control of the current cashflow? Why are they borrowing from an individual and not from their local bank?

Sport Ireland advises against the practice of loans by a director, employee or connected person. If such a loan is made to a sporting entity funded by Sport Ireland it must notify Sport Ireland of the terms, the purpose and the circumstances.

Money Laundering

'Money laundering is the processing of criminal proceeds (cash and assets obtained from criminal activities) to disguise their original origin.'[221] With the growing commercialisation of sport and large money flows, sport can be an effective way of laundering funds.

Sport is vulnerable as it is easy to enter the market, there are lots of different stakeholders and money flows, and, importantly, management may lack professionalism. Many clubs may be financially constrained and their players young and vulnerable.

Illegal activities within a club may not be reported for fear of reputational damage. If a grantor or sponsor hears rumours of poor financial control, they will back off, potentially devastating revenue. Members may lose faith in the leadership. As a result, money laundering and corruption may be more prevalent than reported.

Money laundering can be straightforward and local. It occurs in small entities as well on the international stage. For instance, an amateur club may be regularly in deficit but topped up in cash by a local businessman. The board needs to question the source of funds.

Basic financial controls guard against potential money laundering. The board should ensure that:

- Employees and players are aware of the potential for money laundering
- Only individuals approved by the board can bind the entity
- All accounting records are up to date and board members have the opportunity and knowledge to question transactions
- The identity of counterparties is known and if necessary appropriate enquiries are made

Register of Beneficial Owners

As a result of money laundering legislation a register of beneficial ownership of companies has been set up. It is run by the Companies Registration Office (the CRO). The purpose is to improve transparency by making it clear who ultimately owns or controls Irish companies and thus 'to deter money laundering and terrorist financing and to help sanction those who hide their ownership or control ... for the purpose of facilitating illegal activities.'[222]

Where there is no clear beneficial owner, e.g. in a sporting entity, the CEO or chair should register as the person ultimately controlling the entity, described as the 'managing official'.

INTEGRITY OF SPORT

Betting

Betting has a two-sided relationship with sport. On the one hand, it has long been an important revenue source, but it has also led to match fixing and altering the results of sporting competitions. Betting can be used both for the generation of illegal proceeds from game fixing and for money laundering purposes.

Sport is vulnerable to betting fraud. This is particularly where players are paid relatively little and may be on insecure contracts while matches are televised internationally and huge funds may be being exchanged. Sport based on skill and chance can be particularly susceptible to manipulation and fraud. The bet may be as simple as the issuing of a card. An example of this risk occurred in League of Ireland football when two players were banned for twelve months after an investigation was prompted by unusual betting patterns on a local game.[223]

The board of even small entities needs to be aware of the risk of betting fraud, particularly if their sport is televised. Clear policies and training should be available to players. It should be clear that this 'bit of fun' will not be tolerated. Player contracts should clearly state the penalties for infringing and that a player must never bet on their own game. Some may not see this as wrong, so it is up to the board to ensure that the necessary education is provided. There should be disciplinary rules banning any person from placing a bet on youth leagues or a competition that they can influence. Similarly, the spreading of confidential information that may be used in the framework of a bet should be banned. Any member who is approached with a request to participate in betting fraud should know who to report the approach to.

Cheating

A high-profile case of cheating is the Bloodgate scandal in rugby, where Harlequins faked an injury to bring back an accomplished kicker onto the pitch.[224] Another case was the ball tampering incident in cricket in Australia in March 2018 where the Australian player Cameron Bancroft was caught on camera pulling tape from his pocket and rubbing it on the ball. He claimed that he did not know better and 'just wanted to fit in'.[225] Corruption in sport is an important consideration for any CEO running an entity. Concerns need to be discussed with the board, which in turn must monitor the situation.

Anti-Doping

Doping is against the spirit of sport. Anyone on the board of a sporting entity needs to know the basic rules and where to look for help. Sport Ireland is designated as the national anti-doping organisation for the Republic of Ireland.[226] Northern Ireland falls under the jurisdiction of two national anti-doping organisations:

- Sport Ireland[227]
- UK Anti-Doping[228]

The affiliation structure of Northern Irish sports/branches determines the national anti-doping organisation it falls under and in turn the anti-doping rules which govern the sport. For example, Sport Ireland has jurisdiction for all-Ireland sports, such as rugby, hockey and swimming, while UK Anti-Doping has jurisdiction for sports affiliated to a British governing body or international federation, e.g. judo or the Irish Football Association. Each organisation can drug-test athletes/sports under their jurisdiction in Northern Ireland.

There is pressure for anti-doping control to be separated from the entity that is responsible for high performance and elite athletes. As a result the National Sports Policy aims to:

'Examine the potential for the establishment of an independent anti-doping agency during the first two years of the policy'.[229]

WADA

The World Anti-Doping Agency (WADA) coordinates the global fight against doping in sport. It produces the *World Anti-Doping Code*. This is the document harmonising anti-doping policies in all sports and all countries. It is reflected in the Irish anti-doping rules which can be found on Sport Ireland's website.[230]

Education

To ensure that a sport is drug free requires education. Board members must ensure that their athletes know what substances and methods are on the prohibited list and how to check any medication. The board of a sporting entity should make the resources from WADA and Sport Ireland available to their membership.

Adequate education is essential to eliminate examples of athletes committing an 'inadvertent' violation, whether by using an over-the-counter medication which contains prohibited substances, or from recreational drugs, such as cannabis or cocaine, or from the use of supplements.

In 2018 a boxer was found to have violated the rules by taking cannabis, while in 2016 there was an example of a GAA player who was adamant that he did not know that tablets he was taking contained a prohibited substance. He had not had any anti-doping education and, although taking supplements, had no idea where to look to check if they were prohibited. Education can ensure that such cases do not happen.

Testing

A sporting entity must ensure that its athletes know who might be tested. It should be noted that relatively 'ordinary' athletes can be tested. They might be participating at a national championship or have been on a team list. For instance, a young GAA player had been put on panel for a national league match even though it may have been unlikely that he would have made the county championship side. Nevertheless, he was tested at a training session, tested positive and was found to have shown a high degree of negligence in consuming a tablet without adequate research.

A board member should have a working knowledge of the anti-doping rules.

Animal Doping

Where relevant the board needs to be up to date on doping of animals and welfare issues, for example, the International Federation for Equestrian Sports (FEI) policy on doping of horses. In 2004 an Irish showjumper won a medal at the Summer Olympics but his horse tested positive for a prohibited substance and the rider lost the medal and received a three-month ban.[231] The FEI did find that there was no deliberate attempt to affect the performance of the horse.

Animal welfare is an important area and particularly looking after animals after the end of their sporting career, e.g. re-training race horses. The board should ensure that there is proper education within the sport at all levels to ensure good animal welfare. This issue should be regularly addressed at board level.

THE SMALLER ENTITY

Monitoring People

Volunteers

Every smaller sporting entity relies heavily on volunteers. They must be clear on their role and who they have to answer to.[232] They should always be thanked.

Equality

All board members must be aware of the nine grounds of discrimination and make sure activities are as accessible as possible.[233]

Monitoring Safeguarding Children and Young People

No matter how small the sporting entity the *Safeguarding Guidance* must be adopted and implemented. Everyone involved with children and young people in sport must attend the basic level safeguarding course.

Monitoring Compliance with Legal Obligations

Tax

Sporting entities are only exempt from corporation tax if they have applied to Revenue for an exemption. Any change to their constitution must be approved by Revenue. Donors may give tax-allowable gifts for capital projects, subject to detailed conditions.

PAYE and PRSI are payable on employees. The club should make sure that its expenses policy is clearly documented and acceptable to Revenue, e.g. by using civil service mileage rates.

Monitoring Compliance with Financial Obligations[234]

The board must comply with the terms and conditions of public or private grants received, including governance requirements.[235]

Integrity

Even smaller sporting entities need to be vigilant as to betting practices, corruption and cheating. Cheating can affect any sport at any level, e.g. taking the bus to win a medal in a local marathon.[236] Someone may cheat if they have the opportunity.

Anti-doping education should take place at all levels of the sport, as well as, where relevant, animal welfare training. The board should remind members as to where information can be sought in regard to human doping, and, where relevant, animal doping.

CONCLUSION

Governance of an organisation involves monitoring. The board not only directs but also controls. They must continually review how the organisation is being run by the CEO and senior management and also consider external demands, e.g. company law and tax, and external threats such as betting and doping.

Ten Key Points

1. The CEO runs the sporting entity day-to-day and is responsible for leading management. They ensure that the decisions of the board are communicated to the management team and they report back to the board on the implementation of their decisions. There should be clear terms of reference so that the CEO is accountable but that the board does not encroach on the CEO's role.
2. Managing employees is an exceedingly complex area and is likely to be one of the entity's largest costs, as well as being an area of high risk. Specialist advice is essential to ensure that all legal obligations are complied with.
3. The CEO is responsible for managing volunteers. This is a challenging area. Volunteers are giving their time for free and as a result may not like being held accountable. The

more effort the entity invests in its volunteers the better their accountability is likely to be.

4. Training and upskilling of board members, staff and volunteers contributes to the strength of the entity.

5. The board should monitor equal opportunity and equal treatment in all policies and initiatives and include equality and diversity in its strategy.

6. Every sporting entity must adopt and implement the *Safeguarding Guidance* developed by Sport Ireland and Sport NI. Although not essential for board members who are not involved with children, it is useful for all board members to have attended at least the Level I Safeguarding course so that they understand the key issues. Anyone who is involved in supervision, education or training of children is required to be vetted.

7. All sporting entities that are companies, rather than unincorporated entities, must be compliant with the Companies Act 2014. Every board member declares on their application that they are familiar with their duties under the Companies Act.

8. There is a specific exemption for sporting entities for corporation tax, but this must be applied for and conditions met. VAT and PAYE are still payable.

9. 'Money laundering is the processing of criminal proceeds (cash and assets obtained from criminal activities) to disguise their original origin.' With the growing commercialisation of sport and large money flows, sport risks being an effective way of laundering funds. The board of even small entities needs to be aware of the risk of betting fraud and bribery. Clear policies and training should be available to players.

10. Doping is against the spirit of sport. Sport Ireland is designated as the national anti-doping organisation. The World Anti-Doping Agency (WADA) coordinates the global fight against human doping in sport. It produces the *World Anti-Doping Code* which is the document

harmonising anti-doping policies in all sports and all countries. The board should ensure that members are adequately educated and reminded as to where information can be sought both in regard to human doping, and, where relevant, animal doping.

APPENDIX

INTRODUCTION TO THE SPORTS CODE TYPE A

This appendix sets out the Sports Code as it relates to Type A organisations.

Type A sporting organisations are smaller entities, run by volunteers, and do not employ staff. The board members are responsible for:

1. 'Overseeing the work of the organisation (governance);
2. Organising the daily work (management), and;
3. Carrying out the work of the organisation (operations).'[237]

The sections on smaller entities at the end of each chapter in this book refer specifically to such Type A entities. The code is also referenced in the footnotes.

The provisions for larger sporting organisations, i.e. Type B and Type C, are reflected in the Sports Code Type B and Type C. The provisions for such entities are similar but more detailed and can be found in the Sports Code online.[238]

PRINCIPLE 1: LEADING OUR ORGANISATION

1.1 Agreeing our vision, purpose, mission, values and objectives and making sure that they remain relevant.

1.1(a) Agree the purpose and objectives of your group. Discuss how the group wants to achieve its objectives and how it wants to work.

1.1(b) Write this out in the form of a **constitution** for the organisation.

1.1(c) Review at least every three years to ensure that the organisation is still relevant.

1.1(d) Develop and agree written policies as to how you want things to work where necessary. Review at least every three years.

1.2 Developing, resourcing, monitoring and evaluating a plan so that our organisation achieves its stated purpose and objectives.

1.2(a) Agree and write down a work plan – ideally every year. This plan should have:
- the most important actions to meet objectives;
- timelines to achieve these actions;
- the breakdown of the budget; and
- a description of how the money will be raised.

1.2(b) Agree who is going to take responsibility for the actions to carry out the plan.

1.2(c) Review the plan once a year. Have a discussion about what went well and what could be improved before agreeing a new work plan.

1.3 Managing, supporting and holding to account staff, volunteers and all who act on behalf of the organisation.

1.3(a) Set realistic goals. Divide up the work and review progress of agreed actions at the next meeting.

1.3(b) Chair makes sure that individual board members report to the board on work that they carry out for the organisation.

1.3(c) Where volunteers, who are not on the board, are involved make sure they are clear on their role and who they have to answer to.

PRINCIPLE 2: EXERCISING CONTROL OVER OUR ORGANISATION

2.1 Identifying and complying with all relevant legal and regulatory requirements.

2.1(a) Decide if the group's current legal form is appropriate. For example, is your group:
- an unincorporated association;
- a company limited by guarantee;
- a trust; or
- a friendly society.

Comply with the relevant requirements.

2.1(b) If the group is not a company limited by guarantee, make sure that someone is appointed (usually called a Secretary) to keep track of the group's records, meeting minutes, membership, and so on.

[Principles 2.1(c) and 2.1(d), which deal with charities, are superseded by a new Charities Governance Code, published in November 2018 and overseen by the Charities Regulatory Authority. All charities are expected to have started reporting their compliance with the Charities Governance Code by 2021.]

2.1(e) Make sure that your group is complying with all legal, regulatory and any contractual obligations.

2.1(f) Consider the health and safety aspects of activities.
Put a plan in place to deal with any problems.

2.1(g) Be aware of the nine grounds of discrimination. Make sure activities are as accessible as possible.

2.1(h)

- Keep contact details of stakeholders with their permission in a safe place.
- Do not give their details without their consent to someone outside the group.
- Do not keep unnecessary personal information.
- Make sure your organisation complies with data protection legislation.

2.1(i) Comply with other law that applies to activities of a group (for example, child protection or food safety).

2.1(j) Comply with the terms and conditions of public or private grants received, including governance requirements.

2.2 Making sure there are appropriate internal financial and management controls.

2.2(a) Monitor income and expenditure against the budget on a regular basis.

2.2(b) Draw up a yearly report of income and expenditure.

2.2(c) Agree and put in place appropriate financial management procedures.

2.3 Identifying major risks for our organisation and deciding ways of managing the risks.

2.3(a) Think about problems that may arise, and the risks that may be needed to achieve the organisation's aims.

Agree a yearly plan to deal with major risks.

For example:

- Garda vetting for volunteers if they work with children or vulnerable adults;
- doing regular back-ups of your database or mailing list; and
- monitoring the plans which have been put in place to pay back a bank loan.

2.3(b) Take out appropriate insurance, for example, public liability insurance or buildings insurance.

2.3(c) If your group owns property or any assets, make sure that legal ownership is in the name of the group and that the community interest is protected if the group closes.

Take legal advice if necessary.

PRINCIPLE 3: BEING TRANSPARENT AND ACCOUNTABLE

3.1 Identifying those who have a legitimate interest in the work of our organisation (stakeholders) and making sure there is regular and effective communication with them about our organisation.

3.1(a) Decide who you need to communicate with and how you will do that taking into account your time and financial resources.

3.1(b) Appoint an agreed spokesperson for the group.

3.1(c) Produce a yearly activity report. Make it widely available (for example, on your website if you have one).

3.1(d) Meet the reporting requirements of any funder or relevant regulator.

3.1(e) Hold an annual meeting of members and anyone else who may be interested and report on the activities of the year.

3.2 Responding to stakeholders' questions or views about our organisation's work and how we run it.

3.2(a) Use the annual meeting to listen to people's views about the work of the organisation.

3.2(b) Put a clear system in place for dealing with correspondence, feedback and complaints to the organisation.

3.3 Encouraging and enabling engagement with those who benefit from our organisation in the planning and decision-making of the organisation.

3.3(a) Actively seek feedback from the stakeholders of your group. (This could be done regularly on a word of mouth basis, or you may want to do something more formal such as a yearly survey.)

3.3(b) Use the annual meeting to consult with your stakeholders if you are planning to make significant changes to the way that you do things.

PRINCIPLE 4: WORKING EFFECTIVELY

4.1 Making sure that our governing body, individual board members, committees, staff and volunteers understand their: role, legal duties, and delegated responsibility for decision-making.

4.1(a) Make sure that all board members and sub-committee members (if any) understand and are familiar with the Governance Code [Sports Code] and the constitution.

4.1(b) Make sure that board members understand that while they were nominated by a particular group, they must not act as a representative of that group in acting as a board member. Instead, they should promote the aims of the organisation in line with its governing document. Board members must at all times respect board confidentiality.

4.1(c)   Identify a chair, secretary and treasurer for the group and decide when and how the positions will be rotated.

4.1(d)   Decide and record how decisions will be taken at meetings and between meetings if necessary.

4.2 Making sure that as a board we exercise our collective responsibility through board meetings that are efficient and effective.

4.2(a)   Have regular meetings with sufficient notice.

4.2(b)   Have an agenda for each meeting.

4.2(c)   Take minutes and agree them at the next meeting.

4.2(d)   Start and finish meetings on time.
Chair keeps order at meetings, encourages participation and ensures that decisions are made.

4.3 Continually reviewing board recruitment, development and retirement processes to ensure relevant competencies are in place to realise the organisation's objectives.

4.3(a)   Take time once a year to identify ways in which the working of the board could be improved.

4.3(b)   Take time once a year to discuss who might be interested in joining the board and who might want to leave.
Agree who you would like to invite onto the board, bearing in mind the need for a mix of skills and diversity in terms of background and experience. (Make sure that you follow your own rules about election to the board as laid out in your constitution.) Consider the extent to which your board is made up of member representatives, beneficiaries or external representatives to avoid loyalty dilemmas and decide what the best mix is.

4.3(c)   Welcome new board members, explain the work of the board and its committees and help them to get involved. Make sure they have a copy of the constitution and this Governance Code [Sports Code].

PRINCIPLE 5: BEHAVING WITH INTEGRITY

5.1 Being honest, fair and independent.

5.1(a)   Make sure the chair leads the board in developing an ethical culture in line with the values of the organisation.

5.1(b)   Develop and agree a code of conduct or set ground rules for board or committee members.

5.1(c)   Make sure the code of conduct gives clear guidelines on the receipt of gifts or hospitality by board members.

5.1(d)   Make sure all board members sign a commitment to the code.

5.1(e)   Review your code of conduct at least every three years.

5.1(f)   Be fair by consistently applying the same ethical standards to every person and situation.

5.2 Understanding, declaring and managing conflicts of interest and conflicts of loyalties.

5.2(a)   Hold a discussion about the issues of 'conflict of interest' and 'conflict of loyalty.' Develop a policy on each of these.

5.2(b)   Each board member and anyone else present must tell the board if they believe they have a conflict of interest on a matter to be decided on at a meeting. Unless the board decides otherwise, they must leave when the board is discussing or deciding on that matter. The person concerned should be told what decision was reached.

Conflicts of interest must be recorded in the minutes.

Conflicts of loyalty may be serious enough to be conflicts of interest.

5.3 Protecting and promoting our organisation's reputation.

5.3(a)   Make sure all board members understand their responsibility to act as champions for the group by promoting its work and reputation.

5.3(b)   Make sure the code of conduct clarifies that board members have a duty to maintain the confidentiality of board meetings.

ENDNOTES

[1]   Action 31 of the *National Sports Policy*, p. 69, https://www.gov.ie/en/publication/aaa7d9-national-sports-policy-2018-2027/.

[2]   Play the Game, *The Sports Governance Observer*, playthegame.org/themepages/the-sports-governance-observer/the-sports-governance-observer/.

[3]   https://www.sportireland.ie/national-governing-bodies/governance-0.

[4]   Department of Transport, Tourism and Sport, 'Sport', https://www.gov.ie/en/policy/6d07a6-sport/.

[5]   Sport Ireland, 'Local Sports Partnerships', https://www.sportireland.ie/participation/local-sports-partnerships.

[6]   Sports Governance NI (2017) *Sports Governance Guide Northern Ireland*, http://www.sportsgovernanceni.net/wp-content/uploads/2017/11/Sport-Governance-Guide-2017-Nov-Small.pdf.

[7]   Department of Transport, Tourism and Sport (2018) *National Sports Policy 2018–2027*, p. 56, https://www.gov.ie/en/publication/aaa7d9-national-sports-policy-2018-2027/.

[8]   http://www.sportni.net/about-us/.

[9]   Cambridge Judge Business School, The Cadbury Archive: *The Cadbury Report*, cadbury.cjbs.archios.info.

[10] Sport Ireland (2019) 'Sport Ireland Takes Over Governance Code for Sporting Organisations', 6 June, www.sportireland.ie/news/sport-ireland-takes-over-governance-code-for-sporting-organisations.

[11] Sport England and UK Sport, *A Code for Sports Governance*, www.uksport.gov.uk/resources/governance-code.

[12] Sport Ireland (2019) 'Sport Ireland Takes Over Governance Code for Sporting Organisations', 6 June, www.sportireland.ie/news/sport-ireland-takes-over-governance-code-for-sporting-organisations.

13   Companies Act 2014, section 223(3).
14   *National Sports Policy 2018–2027*, p. 69.
15   Principle 1.2a of the Sports Code (Types A, B and C).
16   Principle 2.1a of the Sports Code (Types A and B).
17   Principle 1.1b of the Sports Code (Type A).
18   Companies Act 2014, sections 169(1) and 1201.
19   Principle 4.1g of the Sports Code (Type C).
20   Companies Act 2014, section 228(1).
21   Principle 4.2d of the Sports Code (Types A, B and C).
22   Principle 2.1b of the Sports Code (Types B and C).
23   Companies Act 2014, section 129(1).
24   Companies Act 2014, section 226.
25   Companies Act 2014, section 129(4).
26   Companies Act 2014, section 129(3).
27   Section 1.19 of *A Code for Sports Governance*, Sport England and UK Sport.
28   *National Sports Policy 2018–2027*, p. 55.
29   Principle 4.1b of the Sports Code (Types A, B and C).
30   Companies Act 2014, section 222.
31   Principle 2.1a of the Sports Code (Types A and B).
32   Principle 1.1b of the Sports Code (Types A, B and C).
33   Principle 2.3b of the Sports Code (Types A, B and C).
34   Principle 4.2d of the Sports Code (Types A, B and C).
35   Principle 4.1b of the Sports Code (Type A).
36   Principles 4.1a and 4.3c of the Sports Code (Types A, B and C).
37   Principles 4.1a and 4.1g of the Sports Code (Type C).
38   Principle 4.1a of the Sports Code (Types A, B and C).
39   OECD's *Principles of Corporate Governance* 1999 (updated 2015), quoted on page 5 of the Sports Code.
40   Principle 4.1a of the Sports Code (Type C).
41   Principle 4.1a of the Sports Code (Type C).
42   Principle 4.1e of the Sports Code (Types B and C).
43   Principles 4.1e and 4.1f of the Sports Code (Types B and C).
44   Principle 4.1a of the Sports Code (Type C).
45   Principle 2.3a of the Sports Code (Types A, B and C).
46   Principle 2.1i of the Sports Code (Types B and C).
47   Principles 5.2a and 5.2b of the Sports Code (Types A, B and C).
48   Principle 4.1b of the Sports Code (Types A, B and C).
49   Principle 2.1h of the Sports Code (Types A, B and C).
50   Principles 1.3a, 1.3b and 2.1g of the Sports Code (Types A, B and C).
51   As defined in Appendix 3 of the Sports Code.
52   Principle 2.1g of the Sports Code (Types A, B and C).

53   Willsher, Kim (2018) 'Paris Saint-Germain Admit to Racially Profiling Young Players', *The Guardian*, 8 November, https://www.theguardian.com/football/2018/nov/08/paris-saint-germain-racial-profiling-black-players.
54   Principle 2.1f of the Sports Code (Types A, B and C).
55   Principle 1.3c of the Sports Code (Types A, B and C).
56   As defined in Appendix 3 of the Sports Code.
57   Principle 2.2e of the Sports Code (Type C).
58   Principles 5.1b and 5.1c of the Sports Code (Types A, B and C).
59   Principle 4.1d of the Sports Code (Type C).
60   Principle 4.2 of the Sports Code (Types A, B and C).
61   Principle 2.2e of the Sports Code (Type C).
62   Principle 2.2 of the Sports Code (Types A, B and C).
63   Principle 4.1c of the Sports Code (Type C).
64   Principle 4.1a and 4.3c of the Sports Code (Type C).
65   Principle 2.3 of the Sports Code (Type A).
66   Principle 2.1i of the Sports Code (Type A).
67   Principle 5.2 of the Sports Code (Type A).
68   Principle 4.1b of the Sports Code (Types A, B and C).
69   Principle 2.1h of the Sports Code (Type A).
70   Principle 2.1g of the Sports Code (Type A).
71   Principle 2.1f of the Sports Code (Type A).
72   Principle 1.3c of the Sports Code (Type A).
73   Principles 5.1b and 5.1c of the Sports Code (Type A).
74   Principle 4.1d of the Sports Code (Type A).
75   Principles 4.2a and 4.2c of the Sports Code (Types A, B and C).
76   Principles 4.2b and 4.2c of the Sports Code (Types A, B and C).
77   Principle 1.2e of the Sports Code (Type C).
78   Principle 3.2c of the Sports Code (Type C).
79   Sport Ireland (2018) *Recognition Criteria for National Governing Bodies of Sport*, https://www.sportireland.ie/sites/default/files/2020-02/sport-ireland-recognition-criteria_0.pdf.
80   *Jacob v Irish Amateur Rowing Union Ltd* [2008] IEHC 196.
81   *Kieran Gould v Michael Sweeney & Others*, High Court, 23 January 2007.
82   *Limerick FC v FAI* [2007] IEHC 67.
83   *Dollingstown Football Club v Irish Football Association* [2011] NIQB 66 (19 August 2011).
84   Principle 4.2d of the Sports Code (Types A, B and C).
85   Principle 2.1e of the Sports Code (Types A, B and C).
86   Principle 4.2c of the Sports Code (Types A, B and C).
87   Principle 4.2c of the Sports Code (Types A, B and C) and Principle 4.2f of the Sports Code (Type C).
88   Principle 4.2 of the Sports Code (Type A).

89 Principle 2.1b of the Sports Code (Type A).
90 *Irish Times* (2014) 'Amateur Golfer Loses Defamation Case after 83 Days in Court', 9 October, https://www.irishtimes.com/news/crime-and-law/courts/amateur-golfer-loses-defamation-case-after-83-days-in-court-1.1958145.
91 Principle 4.3b of the Sports Code (Types A, B and C).
92 Action 31 of the *National Sports Policy 2018–2027*, p. 70.
93 Action 32 of the *National Sports Policy*, p. 71.
94 Principle 4.3a of the Sport Code (Types A, B and C) and Principle 4.3d of the Sports Code (Types B and C).
95 Geeraert, Arnout (ed.) *National Sports Governance Observer Final Report*, November 2018, https://playthegame.org/knowledge-bank/downloads/national-sports-governance-observer-final-report/f80a5652-8ae2-479c-8bb8-a9ad00b3aec7, p. 37.
96 Principle 4.3 of the Sports Code (Type A).
97 Principle 4.3b of the Sports Code (Type A).
98 Principle 4.3a of the Sports Code (Type A).
99 Bull, Andy (2013) 'Death of a Schoolboy: Why Concussion Is Rugby Union's Dirty Secret', *The Guardian*, 13 December, https://www.theguardian.com/sport/2013/dec/13/death-of-a-schoolboy-ben-robinson-concussion-rugby-union.
100 Principle 1.1b of the Sports Code (Types A, B and C).
101 Badminton Ireland (2016) *Badminton Ireland Memorandum of Association*, https://www.badmintonireland.com/file/742152/?dl=1.
102 Principle 1.1a of the Sports Code (Types B and C).
103 IRFU (2018) *Strategic Plan 2018–2023*, https://d2cx26qpfwuhvu.cloudfront.net/irfu/wp-content/uploads/2018/12/19161726/IRFU_Strategic_Plan_2018-2023.pdf.
104 Principle 1.1a of the Sports Code (Types A, B and C).
105 GAA (2018) *Strategic Plan 2018–2021*, p. 14, https://www.gaa.ie/sportteller-content/stories/1/1/4a8c76b2-b2f4-4e04-99cf-bb843699a0b2/index.html#Pages_12-13.
106 GAA (2018) *Strategic Plan 2018–2021*, p. 19, https://www.gaa.ie/sportteller-content/stories/1/1/4a8c76b2-b2f4-4e04-99cf-bb843699a0b2/index.html#Pages_16-17.
107 Olympic Council of Ireland (2017) *Strategic Plan 2018–2024*, p. 2, https://olympics.ie/wp-content/uploads/2017/12/Strategic-Plan-Booklet.pdf.
108 Badminton Ireland (2018) *Badminton Ireland Strategic Plan 2018–2021*, https://www.badmintonireland.com/file/823355/?dl=1 09/01/19.
109 Sport Ireland (2017) *The Rio Review*, https://www.sportireland.ie/sites/default/files/2019-10/rio-review-final.pdf.

[110] Cricket Ireland (2016) *Strategic Plan 2016–2020*, p. 12, http://www.cricket ireland.ie/images/uploads/site_images/Cricket_Ireland_Strategic_Plan. pdf.

[111] Principles 1.1d and 1.2 of the Sports Code (Types A, B and C).

[112] Irish Athletic Boxing Association (2017) *Boxing Clever: 2017–2020 Strategic Plan*, p. 40, http://iaba.ie/site3/wp-content/uploads/2014/10/IABA-Strategic-Plan-2017-2020_WEB.pdf.

[113] Olympic Federation of Ireland (2018) *Annual Report 2018*, p. 19, https://olympics.ie/wp-content/uploads/2019/06/OFI-Annual-Report-Digital.pdf.

[114] Principle 1.2a of the Sports Code (Types A, B and C).

[115] Principle 1.2 of the Sports Code (Types A, B and C).

[116] Cricket Ireland (2016) *Strategic Plan 2016–2020*, p. 26, http://www.cricket ireland.ie/images/uploads/site_images/Cricket_Ireland_Strategic_Plan. pdf.

[117] Principles 3.1, 3.2 and 3.3 of the Sports Code (Types A, B and C).

[118] Sports Code, p. 71.

[119] Principle 1.1a of the Sports Code (Type A).

[120] Principle 1.2a of the Sports Code (Type A).

[121] Principle 1.2b of the Sports Code (Type A).

[122] Principle 1.2c of the Sports Code (Type A).

[123] Principle 1.1c of the Sports Code (Type A).

[124] Principle 1.1d of the Sports Code (Type A)

[125] Principle 2.3a of the Sports Code (Types A, B and C).

[126] Lyons, Eon (2018), 'Bray Wanderers Player Slams Club After Latest Financial Troubles', *Balls.ie*, 3 July, https://www.balls.ie/football/bray-wanderers-financial-woes-deepen-392146; McDonnell, Shane (2014) 'League of Ireland Finances – What Is to Be Done?', *Pundit Arena*, 16 October,http://punditarena.com/irishfootball/smcdonnell2014/league-ireland-finances-done/.

[127] Reid, Philip (2017) 'Participation Rates Fall: Fewer Youths Playing Golf in Ireland', *Irish Times*, 22 May, https://www.irishtimes.com/sport/golf/participation-rates-fall-fewer-youths-playing-golf-in-ireland-1.3091906.

[128] Companies Act 2014, section 281.

[129] Companies Act 2014, section 283.

[130] Companies Act 2014, section 324(6).

[131] Companies Act 2014, section 324(7).

[132] Principles 3.1c, 2.2a and 2.2b of the Sports Code (Types A, B and C).

[133] Companies Act 2014, section 289.

[134] Companies Act 2014, section 321.

[135] Companies Act 2014, section 326330.

[136] Principles 2.2c (Types A, B and C). and 2.2d (Types B and C) of the Sports Code.

137   Principle 2.3c of the Sports Code (Types A, B and C).

138   Article 30(1) of the EU's Fourth Anti-Money Laundering Directive

139   Revenue, 'Sports Body Tax Exemption', https://www.revenue.ie/en/companies-and-charities/charities-and-sports-bodies/sports-bodies-tax-exemption/conditions-for-retaining-the-tax-exemption.aspx.

140   Companies Act 2014, section 334.

141   Companies Act 2014, section 1218.

142   Fogarty, John (2018) 'Galway Clubs Want Answers after "Damning" Audit', *Irish Examiner*, 17 December, https://www.irishexaminer.com/breaking-news/sport/gaa/galway-clubs-want-answers-after-damningaudit-892456.html.

143   Principle 2.3b of the Sports Code (Types A, B and C).

144   *Irish Times* (2014) 'Amateur Golfer Loses Defamation Case after 83 Days in Court', 9 October, https://www.irishtimes.com/news/crime-and-law/courts/amateur-golfer-loses-defamation-case-after-83-days-in-court-1.1958145.

145   Principle 2.3d of the Sports Code (Type C).

146   Principle 2.2 of the Sports Code (Types A, B and C).

147   Principles 2.2a and 2.2b of the Sports Code (Types A, B and C).

148   Principle 2.3 of the Sports Code (Types A, B and C).

149   Principles 3.1a, 3.1b and 3.2c of the Sports Code (Types A, B and C).

150   Principle 3.1f of the Sports Code (Type C).

151   Principle 2.1h of the Sports Code (Types A, B and C).

152   Principle 3.1e of the Sports Code (Types A, B and C).

153   Principle 3.2a of the Sports Code (Types A, B and C).

154   Companies Act 2014, section 178(3).

155   Companies Act 2014, section 181

156   Companies Act 2014, section 181(2)

157   Companies Act 2014, section 181(5).

158   Companies Act 2014, section 146(3).

159   Companies Act 2014, section 396(2).

160   Companies Act 2014, section 218(4).

161   Revenue, 'Travel and Subsistence: Civil Service Rates', https://www.revenue.ie/en/employing-people/employee-expenses/travel-and-subsistence/civil-service-rates.aspx.

162   Principles 5.2a–c of the Sports Code (Types A, B and C).

163   Principle 5.3a of the Sports Code (Types A, B and C).

164   Principle 4.1b of the Sports Code (Types A, B and C).

165   Principles 5.1a–f of the Sports Code (Types A, B and C).

166   Principle 3.1 of the Sports Code (Type A).

167   Principles 3.1a and 3.1b of the Sports Code (Type A).

168   Principle 3.2 of the Sports Code (Type A).

169 Principle 3.3b of the Sports Code (Type A).
170 Principle 5.2a of the Sports Code (Type A).
171 Principle 5.2b of the Sports Code (Type A).
172 Principle 5.3a of the Sports Code (Type A).
173 Principle 5.1a of the Sports Code (Type A).
174 Principle 5.1b of the Sports Code (Type A).
175 Principle 5.1c of the Sports Code (Type A).
176 Principle 5.1d of the Sports Code (Type A).
177 Principle 5.1e of the Sports Code (Type A).
178 Principle 5.1f of the Sports Code (Type A).
179 Principle 5.3b of the Sports Code (Type A).
180 Principles 3.1d, 1.3e and 4.1e of the Sports Code (Type C).
181 Principle 1.3d of the Sports Code (Type C).
182 Revenue, 'Guide to Pay As You Earn (PAYE): Determining the Employment Status of an Individual', https://www.revenue.ie/en/employing-people/becoming-an-employer-and-ongoing-obligations/guide-to-pay-as-you-earn-paye/determining-the-employment-status-of-an-individual.aspx
183 Principle 1.3d of the Sports Code (Type C).
184 Terms of Employment (Information) Act 1994, section 3.
185 Organisation of Working Time Act 1997, updated to 4 March 2019.
186 Companies Act 2014, section 305(1).
187 Unfair Dismissal Acts 1977–2001.
188 Redundancy Payments Act 1967, section 7(2).
189 McDermott, Stephen (2018) 'Gym Worker Who Yawned and "Rolled on Floor" in front of Members Awarded €1,420 for Unfair Dismissal', TheJournal.ie, 20 October, https://www.thejournal.ie/gym-worker-unfair-dismissal-award-wrc-4294756-Oct2018/.
190 Principle 1.3c of the Sports Code (Types A, B and C).
191 Action 27 of the National Sports Policy, p. 67.
192 Action 28 of the National Sports Policy, p. 67.
193 Mullooly, Ciarán (2018), 'Football Referee Injured in Assault after Match in Midlands', RTE.ie, 12 November, https://www.rte.ie/news/leinster/2018/1112/1010274-offaly-referee-assault/.
194 Action 31 of the National Sports Policy, p. 69.
195 Action 33 of the National Sports Policy, p. 72.
196 Action 4 of the National Sports Policy, p. 29.
197 Action 28 of the National Sports Policy, p. 67.
198 Employment Equality Acts 1998 and 2004.
199 Sport Ireland (2019) Sport Ireland Policy on Participation in Sport by People with Disabilities, p. 6, https://www.sportireland.ie/sites/default/files/2019-12/sport-ireland-policy-on-participation-in-sport-by-people-with-disabilities.pdf.

[200]   *National Sports Policy*, p. 43.

[201]   Action 12 of the *National Sports Policy*, p. 37.

[202]   Sport Ireland (2019) 'Sport Ireland Launches New Women in Sport Policy', 6 March, https://www.sportireland.ie/women-in-sport/news/sport-ireland-launches-new-women-in-sport-policy.

[203]   https://20x20.ie/.

[204]   Ross, Will (2016) 'Chelsea Doctor Eva Carneiro Settles Dismissal Case', *BBC News*, 7 June, https://www.bbc.com/news/uk-england-36472713.

[205]   Rees, Paul (2016) 'Joe Marler Handed Two-Game Ban and £20,000 Fine for "Gypsy boy" Comment', *The Guardian*, 5 April, https://www.theguardian.com/sport/2016/apr/05/joe-marler-ban-fine-gypsy-boy-harlequins.

[206]   Pardeen, Nazia (2016) 'Jonás Gutiérrez Wins Case against Newcastle over Cancer Treatment', *The Guardian*, 14 April, https://www.theguardian.com/football/2016/apr/14/jonas-gutierrez-wins-discrimination-claim-against-newcastle-utd.

[207]   Watterson, Johnny (2017) 'Tennis Ireland Found to Have Discriminated in CEO Appointment', *Irish Times*, 6 July, https://www.irishtimes.com/sport/other-sports/tennis-ireland-found-to-have-discriminated-in-ceo-appointment-1.3145852.

[208]   Sport Ireland (2020) *Safeguarding Guidance for Children and Young People in Sport*, https://www.athleticsireland.ie/downloads/other/Sport_Ireland_SafeguardingGuidance.pdf.

[209]   Department of Children and Youth Affairs (2017) *Children First: National Guidance for the Protection and Welfare of Children*, https://www.tusla.ie/uploads/content/Children_First_National_Guidance_2017.pdf.

[210]   Department of Health (Northern Ireland) (2017) *Co-operating to Safeguard Children and Young People in Northern Ireland*, https://www.safeguarding.ie/images/Pdfs/National_legislation-NI/co-operating-safeguard-children-young-people-NI.pdf.

[211]   Sport Ireland (2020) *Safeguarding Guidance for Children and Young People in Sport*, p. 40, https://www.sportireland.ie/sites/default/files/2020-01/safeguarding-guidance.pdf.

[212]   Press Association (2018) 'Former Celtic Boys Club Coach Jailed for Historical Child Abuse', *Irish Examiner*, 5 November, https://www.irishexaminer.com/breakingnews/sport/soccer/former-celtic-boys-club-coach-jailed-forhistorical-child-abuse-883360.html.

[213]   Freeman, Hadley (2018) 'How Was Larry Nassar Able to Abuse So Many Gymnasts for So Long?', *The Guardian*, 26 January, https://www.theguardian.com/sport/2018/jan/26/larry-nassar-abuse-gymnasts-scandal-culture.

[214]   Principle 2.1e of the Sports Code (Types A, B and C).

[215]   http://www.irishstatutebook.ie/eli/2014/act/38/enacted/en/print.html.

[216]   Companies Act 2014, section 286(3).

217   Revenue, 'Sports Bodies Tax Exemption', https://www.revenue.ie/en/companies-and-charities/charities-and-sports-bodies/sports-bodies-tax-exemption/index.aspx.
218   Revenue, 'Tax Relief on Donations to Certain Sports Bodies', https://www.revenue.ie/en/companies-and-charities/charities-and-sports-bodies/tax-relief-on-donations-to-certain-sporting-bodies/index.aspx.
219   Revenue, 'Travel and Subsistence: Civil Service Rates', https://www.revenue.ie/en/employing-people/employee-expenses/travel-and-subsistence/civil-service-rates.aspx.
220   Principle 2.1e of the Sports Code (Types A, B and C).
221   www.antimoneylaundering.gov.ie.
222   rbo.gov.ie/faqs.
223   Anderson, Jack (2017) 'League of Ireland Has a Gambling Problem', Irish Times, 29 September, https://www.irishtimes.com/opinion/league-of-ireland-has-a-gambling-problem-1.3237116.
224   Cleary, Mick (2014) 'Bloodgate: How the Scandal Unfolded When Harlequins Met Leinster in April 2009', The Telegraph, 5 December, https://www.telegraph.co.uk/sport/rugbyunion/european-rugby/11276718/Bloodgate-How-thescandal-unfolded-when-Harlequins-met-Leinster-in-April-2009.html.
225   Australian Associated Press (2018) 'Cameron Bancroft Opens Up on Ball Tampering Scandal and David Warner', The Guardian, 26 December, https://www.theguardian.com/sport/2018/dec/26/cricket-ball-tampering-scandal-i-just-wanted-to-fit-in-says-cameron-bancroft.
226   Sport Ireland Act 2015, section 41.
227   https://www.sportireland.ie/anti-doping.
228   https://www.ukad.org.uk/.
229   Action 41 of the National Sports Policy, p. 87.
230   Sport Ireland (2019) The Irish Anti-Doping Rules 2015 Version 2.0, 1 January, https://www.sportireland.ie/2015-anti-doping-rules.
231   Henry, Alan (2005) 'Drugged Horse Costs Ireland Gold', The Guardian, 28 March, https://www.theguardian.com/sport/2005/mar/28/alanhenry.
232   Principle 1.3c of the Sports Code (Type A).
233   Principle 2.1g of the Sports Code (Type A).
234   Principle 2.1e of the Sports Code (Type A).
235   Principle 2.1j of the Sports Code (Type A).
236   Singh, Anita (2011) 'Marathon Runner Caught Bus to the Finish Line', The Telegraph, 12 October, https://www.telegraph.co.uk/news/newstopics/howaboutthat/8820301/Marathon-runner-caught-bus-to-the-finish-line.html.
237   https://www.governancecode.ie/the-code.html.
238   https://www.governancecode.ie/the-code.html.

REFERENCES

20×20, https://20×20.ie/.

Anderson, Jack (2017) 'League of Ireland Has a Gambling Problem', *Irish Times*, 29 September, https://www.irishtimes.com/opinion/league-of-ireland-has-a-gambling-problem-1.3237116.

Australian Associated Press (2018) 'Cameron Bancroft Opens Up on Ball Tampering Scandal and David Warner', *The Guardian*, 26 December, https://www.theguardian.com/sport/2018/dec/26/cricket-ball-tampering-scandal-i-just-wanted-to-fit-in-says-cameron-bancroft.

Badminton Ireland (2016) *Badminton Ireland Memorandum of Association*, https://www.badmintonireland.com/file/742152/?dl=1.

Badminton Ireland (2018) *Badminton Ireland Strategic Plan 2018–2021*, https://www.badmintonireland.com/file/823355/?dl=1 09/01/19.

Bull, Andy (2013) 'Death of a Schoolboy: Why Concussion Is Rugby Union's Dirty Secret', *The Guardian*, 13 December, https://www.theguardian.com/sport/2013/dec/13/death-of-a-schoolboy-ben-robinson-concussion-rugby-union.

Cambridge Judge Business School, *The Cadbury Archive: The Cadbury Report*, cadbury.cjbs.archios.info.

Cleary, Mick (2014) 'Bloodgate: How the Scandal Unfolded When Harlequins Met Leinster in April 2009', *The Telegraph*, 5 December, https://www.telegraph.co.uk/sport/rugbyunion/european-rugby/11276718/Bloodgate-How-thescandal-unfolded-when-Harlequins-met-Leinster-in-April-2009.html.

Cricket Ireland (2016) *Strategic Plan 2016–2020*, http://www.cricketire-land.ie/images/uploads/site_images/Cricket_Ireland_Strategic_Plan. pdf.

Department of Children and Youth Affairs (2017) *Children First: National Guidance for the Protection and Welfare of Children*, https://www.tusla. ie/uploads/content/Children_First_National_Guidance_2017.pdf.

Department of Health (Northern Ireland) (2017) *Co-operating to Safe-guard Children and Young People in Northern Ireland*, https://www. safeguarding.ie/images/Pdfs/National_legislation-NI/co-operating-safeguard-children-young-people-NI.pdf.

Department of Justice and Equality, *Anti-Money Laundering Compliance Unit*, http://www.antimoneylaundering.gov.ie/.

Department of Transport, Tourism and Sport (2018) *National Sports Policy 2018–2027*, https://www.gov.ie/en/publication/aaa7d9-national-sports-policy-2018-2027/.

Department of Transport, Tourism and Sport, 'Sport', https://www.gov. ie/en/policy/6d07a6-sport/.

Dollingstown Football Club v Irish Football Association [2011] NIQB 66 (19 August 2011).

Freeman, Hadley (2018) 'How Was Larry Nassar Able to Abuse So Many Gymnasts for So Long?', *The Guardian*, 26 January, https://www. theguardian.com/sport/2018/jan/26/larry-nassar-abuse-gymnasts-scandal-culture.

GAA (2018) *Strategic Plan 2018–2021*, https://www.gaa.ie/sportteller-content/stories/1/1/4a8c76b2-b2f4-4e04-99cf-bb843699a0b2/index. html.

Geeraert, Arnout (ed.) *National Sports Governance Observer Final Report*, November 2018, https://playthegame.org/knowledge-bank/ downloads/national-sports-governance-observer-final-report/f80a5652-8ae2-479c-8bb8-a9ad00b3aec7, p. 37.

Government of Ireland (1967) *Redundancy Payments Act*, http://www. irishstatutebook.ie/eli/1967/act/21/enacted/en/html.

Government of Ireland (1977–2001) *Unfair Dismissal Acts*.

Government of Ireland (1994) *Terms of Employment (Information) Act*, http://www.irishstatutebook.ie/eli/1994/act/5/enacted/en/html.

Government of Ireland (1997) *Organisation of Working Time Act*, updated to 4 March 2019, http://revisedacts.lawreform.ie/eli/1997/act/20/ revised/en/pdf.

Government of Ireland (1998) *Employment Equality Act*, http://www.irishstatutebook.ie/eli/1998/act/21/enacted/en/html.

Government of Ireland (2004) *Employment Equality Act*, http://www.irishstatutebook.ie/eli/2004/act/24/enacted/en/html.

Government of Ireland (2014) *Companies Act*, http://www.irishstatutebook.ie/eli/2014/act/38/enacted/en/html

Government of Ireland (2015) *Sport Ireland Act* 2015, http://www.irishstatutebook.ie/eli/2015/act/15/enacted/en/html.

Henry, Alan (2005) 'Drugged Horse Costs Ireland Gold', *The Guardian*, 28 March, https://www.theguardian.com/sport/2005/mar/28/alanhenry.

Institute of Directors in Ireland, Article 30(1) of the EU's *Fourth Anti-Money Laundering Directive*, https://www.iodireland.ie/resources-policy/legislation/eu's-fourth-anti-money-laundering-directive.

IRFU (2018) *Strategic Plan 2018–2023*, https://d2cx26qpfwuhvu.cloudfront.net/irfu/wp-content/uploads/2018/12/19161726/IRFU_Strategic_Plan_2018-2023.pdf.

Irish Athletic Boxing Association (2017) *Boxing Clever: 2017–2020 Strategic Plan*, http://iaba.ie/site3/wp-content/uploads/2014/10/IABA-Strategic-Plan-2017-2020_WEB.pdf.

Irish Times (2014) 'Amateur Golfer Loses Defamation Case after 83 Days in Court', 9 October, https://www.irishtimes.com/news/crime-and-law/courts/amateur-golfer-loses-defamation-case-after-83-days-in-court-1.1958145.

Jacob v Irish Amateur Rowing Union Ltd [2008] IEHC 196.

John Fogarty (2018) 'Galway Clubs Want Answers after "Damning" Audit', *Irish Examiner*, 17 December, https://www.irishexaminer.com/breakingnews/sport/gaa/galway-clubs-want-answers-after-damnin-gaudit-892456.html.

Kieran Gould v Michael Sweeney & Others, High Court, 23 January 2007.

Limerick FC v FAI [2007] IEHC 67.

Lyons, Eon (2018), 'Bray Wanderers Player Slams Club After Latest Financial Troubles', *Balls.ie*, 3 July, https://www.balls.ie/football/bray-wanderers-financial-woes-deepen-392146.

McDermott, Stephen (2018) 'Gym Worker Who Yawned and "Rolled on Floor" in Front of Members Awarded €1,420 for Unfair Dismissal', *TheJournal.ie*, 20 October, https://www.thejournal.ie/gym-worker-unfair-dismissal-award-wrc-4294756-Oct2018/.

McDonnell, Shane (2014) 'League of Ireland Finances – What Is to Be Done?', *Pundit Arena*, 16 October,http://punditarena.com/irishfootball/smcdonnell2014/league-ireland-finances-done/.

Mullooly, Ciarán (2018), 'Football Referee Injured in Assault after Match in Midlands', *RTE.ie*, 12 November, https://www.rte.ie/news/leinster/2018/1112/1010274-offaly-referee-assault/.

Olympic Council of Ireland (2017) *Strategic Plan 2018–2024*, https://olympics.ie/wp-content/uploads/2017/12/Strategic-Plan-Booklet.pdf.

Olympic Federation of Ireland (2018) *Annual Report 2018*, https://olympics.ie/wp-content/uploads/2019/06/OFI-Annual-Report-Digital.pdf.

Pardeen, Nazia (2016) 'Jonás Gutiérrez Wins Case against Newcastle over Cancer Treatment', *The Guardian*, 14 April, https://www.theguardian.com/football/2016/apr/14/jonas-gutierrez-wins-discrimination-claim-against-newcastle-utd.

Play the Game, *The Sports Governance Observer*, playthegame.org/theme-pages/the-sports-governance-observer/the-sports-governance-observer/.

Press Association (2018) 'Former Celtic Boys Club Coach Jailed for Historical Child Abuse', *Irish Examiner*, 5 November, https://www.irishexaminer.com/breakingnews/sport/soccer/former-celtic-boys-club-coach-jailed-forhistorical-child-abuse-883360.html.

Rees, Paul (2016) 'Joe Marler Handed Two-Game Ban and £20,000 Fine for "Gypsy Boy" Comment', *The Guardian*, 5 April, https://www.theguardian.com/sport/2016/apr/05/joe-marler-ban-fine-gypsy-boy-harlequins.

Reid, Philip (2017) 'Participation Rates Fall: Fewer Youths Playing Golf in Ireland', *Irish Times*, 22 May, https://www.irishtimes.com/sport/golf/participation-rates-fall-fewer-youths-playing-golf-in-ireland-1.3091906.

Revenue, 'Guide to Pay As You Earn (PAYE): Determining the Employment Status of an Individual', https://www.revenue.ie/en/employing-people/becoming-an-employer-and-ongoing-obligations/guide-to-pay-as-you-earn-paye/determining-the-employment-status-of-an-individual.aspx.

Revenue, 'Sports Body Tax Exemption', https://www.revenue.ie/en/companies-and-charities/charities-and-sports-bodies/sports-bodies-tax-exemption/conditions-for-retaining-the-tax-exemption.aspx.

Revenue, 'Tax Relief on Donations to Certain Sports Bodies', https://www.revenue.ie/en/companies-and-charities/charities-and-sports-bodies/tax-relief-on-donations-to-certain-sporting-bodies/index.aspx.

Revenue, 'Travel and Subsistence: Civil Service Rates', https://www.revenue.ie/en/employing-people/employee-expenses/travel-and-subsistence/civil-service-rates.aspx.

Ross, Will (2016) 'Chelsea Doctor Eva Carneiro Settles Dismissal Case', *BBC News*, 7 June, https://www.bbc.com/news/uk-england-36472713.

Singh, Anita (2011) 'Marathon Runner Caught Bus to the Finish Line', *The Telegraph*, 12 October, https://www.telegraph.co.uk/news/newstopics/howaboutthat/8820301/Marathon-runner-caught-bus-to-the-finish-line.html.

Sport England and UK Sport, *A Code for Sports Governance*, www.uksport.gov.uk/resources/governance-code.

Sport Ireland (2017) *The Rio Review*, https://www.sportireland.ie/sites/default/files/2019-10/rio-review-final.pdf.

Sport Ireland (2018) *Recognition Criteria for National Governing Bodies of Sport*, https://www.sportireland.ie/sites/default/files/2020-02/sport-ireland-recognition-criteria_0.pdf.

Sport Ireland (2019) 'Sport Ireland Launches New Women in Sport Policy', 6 March, https://www.sportireland.ie/women-in-sport/news/sport-ireland-launches-new-women-in-sport-policy.

Sport Ireland (2019) *The Irish Anti-Doping Rules 2015 Version 2.0*, 1 January, https://www.sportireland.ie/2015-anti-doping-rules.

Sport Ireland (2019) 'Sport Ireland Takes Over Governance Code for Sporting Organisations', 6 June, www.sportireland.ie/news/sport-ireland-takes-over-governance-code-for-sporting-organisations.

Sport Ireland (2019) *Sport Ireland Policy on Participation in Sport by People with Disabilities*, https://www.sportireland.ie/sites/default/files/2019-12/sport-ireland-policy-on-participation-in-sport-by-people-with-disabilities.pdf.

Sport Ireland (2020) *Safeguarding Guidance for Children and Young People in Sport*, https://www.sportireland.ie/sites/default/files/2020-01/safeguarding-guidance.pdf.

Sport Ireland, 'Local Sports Partnerships', https://www.sportireland.ie/participation/local-sports-partnerships.

Sports Code (Types A, B and C), October 2016, https://www.governancecode.ie/the-code.html.

Sports Governance NI (2017) *Sports Governance Guide Northern Ireland*, http://www.sportsgovernanceni.net/wp-content/uploads/2017/11/Sport-Governance-Guide-2017-Nov-Small.pdf.

UK Anti-Doping (UKAD), https://www.ukad.org.uk/.

Watterson, Johnny (2017) 'Tennis Ireland Found to Have Discriminated in CEO Appointment', *Irish Times*, 6 July, https://www.irishtimes.com/sport/other-sports/tennis-ireland-found-to-have-discriminated-in-ceo-appointment-1.3145852.

Willsher, Kim (2018) 'Paris Saint-Germain Admit to Racially Profiling Young Players', *The Guardian*, 8 November, https://www.theguardian.com/football/2018/nov/08/paris-saint-germain-racial-profiling-black-players.

INDEX

20x20 158, 190

accountability 10, 15, 42, 50, 52,
    59, 60, 82, 85, 87, 110, 111, 118,
    131, 146, 150, 155, 174
    for risk 110
advice 52, 64, 73, 84, 123, 150,
    151, 152, 173, 179
    access to 73
age (grounds for discrimination)
    153, 157
AGM see annual general meeting
alternate board member 33
animal doping 171, 173, 175
annual general meeting 79, 121,
    133, 134, 135, 136, 137, 146
annual report 9, 52, 120, 187
anti-doping 7, 98, 133, 169, 170,
    171, 173, 174, 175, 191
athlete welfare 98, 154
audit committee 53, 54, 55, 58,
    60, 106, 107, 119, 120, 121, 128
audit exemption 118, 144

Badminton Ireland 94, 95, 186
balanced board 77, 78, 85
Bancroft, Cameron 169, 191
behaviour at meetings 70
betting 11, 143, 168, 169, 173, 174,
    see also gambling
board confidentiality 34, 46, 69,
    84, 131, 141–142, 146, 180, 182
board meetings, attendance at
    52, 62–68, 74, 75, 133, 138, 149,
    181
board meetings, behaviour at
    70–72, 74, 75
board members 8, 11, 12, 13
    alternate 33
    communication with 127, see
        also communication
    de facto 34, 37
    duties of 29, 40, 125, 141,
        164
    executive 28, 33
    independent 31–32, 37, 57
    liabilities of 9, 24, 25, 27, 34,
        35, 84, 107, 113, 129

nominee 33–34, 36
non-executive 32, 33, 57,
     119, 133
representative 33–34, 36,
     77, 79, 81, 180, 181
board minutes 73, 75
board policies 45–49, 59
board review committee 56
board size 76, 83
borrowing 117, 166
bribery 49, 139, 174
budgets 54, 70, 89, 95–100, 104
bullying 47, 66, 143, 153, 154

Cadbury, Sir Adrian 8
Carneiro, Eva 158
Celtic Boys' Club 162
CEO 12, 14, 28, 30, 31, 33, 42,
     43, 50, 51, 56, 63, 71, 83, 97,
     138, 148, 149, 150, 152, 153,
     154, 155, 157, 158, 163, 164,
     166, 168, 169, 173, 190
chair 9, 10, 21, 22, 24, 28, 30, 31,
     36, 37, 42, 43, 45, 49, 51, 52, 54,
     57, 61, 62, 63, 67, 68, 69, 70, 71,
     72, 73, 74, 75, 82, 84, 119, 120,
     133, 134, 135, 136, 138, 144,
     145, 146, 149, 168, 177, 181,
     182,
Chelsea 158
chief executive officer, see CEO
Child and Family Agency 160, see
     also Tusla
Children First 159, 161, 190
Children First Act 2015 161
children's officers 160, 161
civil status 157
clg see company limited by
     guarantee

CO, see children's officers
Code for Sports Governance, A
     10, 32, 78, 183, 184
code of conduct 40, 45, 58, 72,
     144, 145, 146, 147, 151, 182
collective responsibility 51, 74,
     181
committees 28, 30, 31, 38, 39, 50,
     52, 53, 54, 57, 58, 60, 64, 70,
     72, 73, 82, 90, 93, 96, 110, 115,
     116, 120, 128, 133, 140, 180, 181
communication 10, 14, 64, 78, 93,
     98, 110, 116, 127, 130, 144
Companies Act 2014 25, 29, 31,
     37, 135, 163, 174, 184, 187–189,
     190
Companies Registration Office 8,
     40, 52, 125, 126, 150, 164
company law 26, 29, 55, 117, 146,
     148, 163, 164, 173
company limited by guarantee 25,
     26, 27, 118, 163, 178
company secretary 21, 31, 37, 63,
     73, 164,
complaints 35, 65, 132, 145, 180
compliance with the Sports Code
     42, 133, 134
Comptroller and Auditor General
     118
confidentiality 34, 45, 46, 58, 69,
     84, 131, 141, 142, 146, 180, 182
confidentiality policy 46, 58, 69,
     84, 141–142, 146, 180, 182
conflict of interests 34, 46, 140,
     145, 147, 182
conflict of loyalty 46, 77, 140,
     145, 147, 181, 182, see also
     conflict of interest

constitution 8, 11, 25, 26–27, 29,
30, 34, 35, 39, 40, 42, 45, 50,
58, 62, 71, 75, 77, 79, 80, 81,
83, 85, 89, 91, 92, 103, 104, 114,
133, 135, 136, 137, 142, 146,
150, 164, 165, 172, 177, 180,
181
consultant 81, 85, 90, 96, 115,
150–151
continuity plans 106, 126, 127, 130
controls 12, 17, 44, 52, 53, 54, 55,
58, 68, 73, 106, 107, 109, 111,
114–117, 118, 119, 120, 128, 129,
167, 168, 173, 179
Co-operating to Safeguard Children
and Young People in Northern
Ireland 159, 190
Court of Arbitration for Sport 7
credit cards 47, 119, 138
Cricket Ireland 95, 100, 187
CRO see Companies Registration
Office
culture 6, 61, 73–74, 142, 144,
145, 146, 155, 182, 190

D&O see directors' and officers'
insurance
data protection 47, 55, 56, 58, 66,
70, 85, 108, 125, 127, 128, 143,
178, see also GDPR
dates of board meetings 62–63, 75
de facto board member 34, 37
Department of Transport,
Tourism and Sport 4, 165, 183
designated liaison person 160, 161
directors' and officers' insurance
27, 123–124
disability 90, 155, 156, 157, 158
disability awareness 155, 156

disaster recovery 106, 107, 126,
127, 128, 130
disciplinary action 26, 47, 49, 56,
65–67, 138, 151
disciplinary issues 24, 63
disciplinary procedure 47, 49, 138
disciplinary policy 49, 65
discrimination 47, 84, 115, 157,
158, 178, 190
dismissal 152, 153, 189, 190
diversification 80, 81, 86, 157
diversity of leadership 156
DLP see designated liaison person
Dollingstown Football Club v Irish
Football Association 67
donations 54, 114, 131, 132, 139,
165, 191
donors 41, 65, 101, 102, 118, 127,
172
due diligence 22, 23, 28, 35, 37,
43, 44, 166
duties of a director 36

education 5, 98, 110, 154, 156,
162, 169, 170, 171, 173, 174
EGM see extraordinary general
meeting
elections to the board 8, 27,
79–80, 81, 136, 181
elite athletes 41, 90, 101, 102,
133, 140, 152, 170
employee contract 151
employer's liability 122
employment policy 47
equality 45, 47, 56, 58, 80, 133,
157, 158, 172, 174, 189
equality policy 47
ethics 40, 48, 59, 132, 142, 143,
144, 147

European Olympic Committee 6
evaluation of the board 76, 81, 82, 85, 86
executive board member 28, 33
exercising control 10, 16, 178
expenses policy 131, 138, 142, 147, 172
external auditor 53, 58, 106, 107, 117, 121
external influencers 89, 100, 132
extraordinary general meeting 91, 135, 136

facilities management 63, 67
factions 70, 71, 74
FAI see Football Association of Ireland
family status 157
Federation of Irish Sport 6
FEI see International Federation for Equestrian Sports
fiduciary duties 14, 29, 37, 40, 125, 141, 156, 164
finance committee 53, 54, 60
finances 25, 26, 44, 59, 63, 64, 95, 99, 104, 187
financial board member 44, 59, 111, 129
financial controls 12, 17, 43, 44, 53, 111, 120, 129, 167
financial performance 53, 111, 120, 129
financial policy 47
financial position 22, 24, 35, 37, 39, 43, 64, 111, 112
financial reporting 24, 47, 53, 107, 121, 143
financial responsibility 54, 120, 129, see also responsibility

financial risk 108, 151
financial statements 44, 50, 53, 111, 112, 113, 114, 117, 120, 133, 136, 144, 152
Football Association of Ireland 7, 11, 32, 185
force majeure 108, 153
founder members 71, 74
funding 4, 13, 25, 42, 63, 77, 90, 95, 96, 97, 98, 103, 108, 117, 142

GAA 7, 93, 170, 171, 186
gambling 110, 117, 143, 168–169, 191 see also betting
garda vetting 70, 179
Gateway team 160
GDPR 47, 70, 84, 134, 156
gender 47, 80, 157
general meeting 91, 121, 135, 137, 142, 146, 198
gifts 48, 131, 132, 139, 143, 145, 147, 172, 182
governance 1, 3–17, 22, 24, 26, 28, 30, 32, 34, 36, 40–42, 44, 46, 48, 50, 52–56, 58, 60, 62–64, 66, 68, 70, 72–74, 77–82, 84, 86, 90, 92–96, 98, 100, 102, 104, 107, 108, 110, 112, 114–116, 118, 120, 122, 124–126, 128, 130, 132–134, 136, 138, 140, 142, 144, 146, 150, 152, 154–156, 158, 160, 162, 164, 166, 168, 170, 172–174, 176, 178, 180, 181, 183, 184, 186
    Code 3–4, 9–10, 11, 41, 73, 178, 180, 181, 183
    guide to 4
    Sports Code 9, 64, see also Sports Code

Governance Code for Community, Voluntary and Charitable Organisations in Ireland 9
governance committee 55, 79
grants 24, 54, 65, 70, 98, 165, 166, 172, 178
grievance procedure 56, 151
group think 69, 73, 75
Gutiérrez, Jonás 158, 190

harassment 47, 143, 153
Harlequins Rugby Club 158, 169
health and safety 24, 45, 48, 58, 63, 70, 81, 85, 107, 108, 110, 116, 124, 133, 141, 156, 166, 178
health and safety aspects of activities 48, 178
health and safety equipment 166
health and safety policy 48
health and safety rules 124, 155
Hermitage Golf Club 74, 125
hidden remuneration 139
high performance 26, 53, 57, 94, 95, 170
horse racing 9, 33
Horse Sport Ireland 102
hospitality 48, 142, 143, 145, 182
human resource risk 109
human resources (HR) committee 56

independence 53, 77, 121
independent board members 31–32, 37, 57
induction 33, 38, 39, 40, 41, 42, 43, 44, 47, 48, 57, 59, 62, 81, 154
information risk 108–109, 141–142, 178

insurance 25, 27, 28, 36, 37, 55, 67, 98, 106, 107, 110, 121, 122, 123, 124, 125, 127, 128, 130, 179
internal audit 53, 119, 121, 128, 129, 152
International Federation for Equestrian Sports 171
International Olympic Committee 5
IRFU see Irish Rugby Football Union
Irish Amateur Swimming Association 109
Irish Athletic Boxing Association 97, 187
Irish Football Association 170, 185
Irish Rugby Football Union 7, 92–93, 186, see also IRFU
Irish Sports Council 4

Jacob v Irish Amateur Rowing Union Ltd 185
joining the board 22, 38–60, 181

Kearns, Daniel 7
key performance indicator 64, 89, 90, 91, 97, 99–100, 104, 113, 129, see also KPI
KPI see key performance indicator

leadership 5, 12, 51, 80, 84, 92, 146, 156, 158, 167
league 13, 15, 168, 169, 171, 187, 191
League of Ireland football 168
leaving the board 76, 84, 86
Lee, Samson 158
length of service 76, 83

letter of appointment 40, 59, 85
limited liability company 25, 27,
    163, see also Ltd
local sports partnerships 5, 15,
    183, see also LSP
LSP 5, 6, 15, 155, 158, see also
    local sports partnerships
Ltd 25, 27, see also limited liability
    company

Magheracloone Gaelic Football
    Club 108
management accounts 113, 129
managing 13, 43, 177, 179, 182
    employees 150, 172, 173,
        177
    official 40
    risk 55, 110
    volunteers 154, 172, 177
Marler, Joe 158, 190
matters reserved for the board
    38, 49, 50, 56, 59
measuring success 64, 89, 99, 113
membership issues 63, 64
membership risk 108
Michigan State University 163
mileage 138
minutes 31, 63, 72, 73, 74, 75,
    133, 138, 145, 178, 181, 182
mission 7, 89, 92, 93, 94, 103,
    104, 115, 117, 153, 154, 177, 178
money laundering 40, 49, 167,
    168, 174, 188
Mourinho, José 158
Mulvey, Kieran 10

Nassar, Larry 163, 190
National Child Abuse Investigation
    Unit 162

national governing bodies 4, 5, 6,
    7, 11, 13, 14, 15, 16, 25, 64, 66,
    80, 93, 98, 100, 101, 102, 109,
    123, 150, 155, 156, 158, 160,
    161, 162, 185
National Sports Governance
    Observer 82, 186
National Sports Policy 2018–2027
    4, 7, 9, 12, 15, 32, 80, 90, 155,
    156, 157, 170, 183, 184, 186,
    189, 190, 191
National Vetting Bureau 161, 162
need for a strategy 89, 90
Newcastle United Football Club
    158
NGB see national governing
    bodies
nomination committee 50, 57
nominee board member 33, 36
non-executive board member 32,
    33, 57, 119, 137
notice of general meetings 137
NVB see National Vetting Bureau

O'Rourke, Derek 109
objects in the constitution 26–27,
    41, 42, 91–92, 103–104, 177,
    181
OFI see Olympic Federation of
    Ireland
Olympic Federation of Ireland 5,
    6, 16, 32, 94, 98, 108, 134, 154,
    187, see also OFI
operational risk 108

Paralympics Ireland 5, 6
PAYE 109, 150, 165, 172, 174, 189
personal accident cover 122
personal sporting disputes 66–67

Play the Game 183
pregnancy 153
president 30, 31
professional development 81, 86, 156
professional indemnity insurance 123
property insurance 123
protected disclosure 153
Protected Disclosures Act 2014 153
provision of loans 166
proxy/proxies 135, 136, 137
PRSI 150, 172
public liability 27, 35, 122, 179

race 80, 153, 157, 171
recommended practice 9, 10, 13, 55, 140
recruitment to the board 70, 76, 77–81, 84, 85, 181
reducing risk 109, 110
redundancy 152, 153, 189
referees 53, 56, 57, 155, 165, 189
register of beneficial owners 40, 168
register of directors 40
register of members 26, 40
religion 157
remuneration 56, 121, 133, 136, 138, 139, 152
remuneration committee 56
representative board member 33–34, 36, 77, 79, 81, 180, 181
reputational risk 109
responsibility 10, 12, 42, 51, 52, 54, 56, 69, 72, 74, 103, 118, 120, 124, 135, 144, 145, 154, 177, 180, 181, 182
Rio Review 95, 186

risk 10, 11, 12, 15, 16, 17, 24, 25, 27, 30, 39, 42, 44, 48, 52, 53, 55, 59, 69, 70, 78, 83, 85, 87, 106, 107, 108, 109, 110, 111, 113, 115, 117, 119, 120, 121, 123, 124, 125, 126, 127, 128, 129, 130, 150, 151, 156, 161, 168, 173, 174, 198
risk assessment 48, 107, 124, 128, 129, 156, 161
risk committee 55, 110, 111
risk management 10, 53, 55, 70, 78, 106, 107, 120, 121, 128, 130
risks associated with not incorporating 28, 106, 125
risk, types of 108
Robinson, Benjamin 85
role of monitor 152
role of the board 39, 42, 43, 51, 52, 59, 96, 98, 104, 115, 117
role of the chair 42, 61, 62, 68, 75
role of the company secretary 31
rotation 71, 72, 76, 83, 84, 85
rules committee 55

safeguarding children 24, 53, 57, 58, 65, 70, 85, 122, 128, 133, 148, 156, 159, 172
Safeguarding Guidance for Children and Young People in Sport 159, 160, 190
safeguarding training 161
SDSI see Sport Dispute Solutions Ireland
section 228 of the Companies Act 2014 29, 164, 184
segregation of duties 116
separation of the executive and non-executive 43

sexual orientation 153, 157
skills of a balanced board 77
Smaller Entity 3
solvency 24, 28, 37, 43, 73, 143, 163
sponsorship 64, 90, 96, 98, 102, 128, 139
Sport Dispute Solutions Ireland 6–7, 66
Sport Ireland 3, 4, 5, 7, 9, 10, 12, 13, 15, 16, 25, 30, 56, 66, 90, 95, 102, 118, 155, 156, 157, 159, 161, 167, 169, 170, 174, 183, 185, 186, 189, 190, 191
    audits 25, 118
    empowering sport organisations 12
    funding from 9, 16, 24, 90, 102, 118, 157, 167
Sport Ireland Act 2015 4, 191
Sport Ireland Coaching 155
Sport Ireland Organisational Development and Change Unit 13, 156
Sport NI see Sport Northern Ireland
Sport Northern Ireland 7, 159, 174
sporting committees 57
Sports Body Tax Exemption 44, 56, 117, 164–165, 172, 174, 188, 191
Sports Code 3, 4, 9, 10, 12, 13, 14, 15, 16, 39, 41, 42, 55, 58, 59, 64, 77, 78, 81, 114, 119, 125, 133, 134, 140, 156, 176, 180, 181, 184–191
    adoption of 4, 12, 13, 156
stakeholder information 134

stakeholders 6, 7, 9, 11, 41, 45, 46, 50, 57, 65, 77, 82, 89, 100, 101, 105, 110, 113, 115, 127, 131, 132, 133, 134, 138, 141, 144, 145, 146, 151, 154, 158, 167, 178, 179, 180, 198
    accounting to 131, 132, 144
statutory auditor 118
strategic plan 6, 46, 64, 80, 82, 90, 91, 92, 93–98, 103, 104, 105, 115, 150
    implementing of 96–98
strategic risk 108
strategy 23, 24, 30, 39, 42, 49, 52, 59, 64, 70, 74, 82, 85, 86, 87, 89, 90, 91, 92, 93, 94, 95, 96, 97, 98, 99, 100, 101, 103, 104, 105, 108, 133, 150, 156, 157, 174
succession 76, 77, 80, 81, 109
    board members 57, 76, 77
    planning 109
Summer Olympics 8, 94, 171
Swim Ireland 109
systems 9, 12, 14, 17, 53, 106, 107, 114, 118, 120, 124, 127

Talbot, Thomas 74, 125
tax 44, 56, 103, 109, 117, 138, 143, 148, 164–165, 172, 173, 174, 188, 191
tax compliance 109
tax relief on donations 165, 191
Tennis Ireland 158, 190
term limits 83
terms of reference 28, 30, 31, 42, 43, 45, 50, 52, 54, 56, 60, 62, 68, 71, 75, 82, 83, 133, 146, 150, 173
terms of reference for the CEO 42

terms of reference of the board
28, 62, 75, 83, 133
time 23
Torbett, James 162
training 12, 13, 14, 29, 47, 50, 53,
56, 64, 70, 76, 77, 81, 82, 85,
90, 94, 97, 98, 100, 110, 111,
123, 155, 156, 161, 162, 168,
171, 173, 174
transparency 10, 15, 52, 73, 78,
95, 114, 118, 132, 133–134, 142,
144, 154, 166, 168,
travel and subsistence, civil
service rates 138, 165, 172,
188, 191
travel insurance 123
Traveller community, membership
of 153, 157
Treacy, John 12
trustees 21, 34, 35, 36, 37, 125
Tusla 65, 160
Type A organisation 9, 15, 58,
176, 184–191
Type B organisation 9, 176,
184–191
Type C organisation 9, 176,
184–191

UK Anti-Doping 169, 170
UK Code for Sports Governance 10,
32, 78

understanding the accounts 106,
111, 128
unincorporated association 178
unincorporated entity 8, 25–28,
37, 80, 113, 117, 136
unincorporated structure 8
US Safe Sport Policy 163
USA Gymnastics 163

validation 156
VAT 174
vetting 70, 161, 162, 179
vision 42, 47, 70, 71, 89, 92, 93,
94, 102 ,103, 104, 124, 142, 149,
155, 156, 162, 166, 174, 176, 177
volunteer 12, 13, 23, 30, 31, 41,
43, 48, 49, 58, 70, 74, 79, 82,
90, 93, 94, 97, 98, 114, 115, 116,
124, 154, 155, 156, 157, 172,
173, 174, 176, 177, 179, 180
volunteer referee 155

WADA 170, 174
whistleblowing 11, 48, 56, 121,
142, 151, 153
whistleblowing policy 48
Women in Sport 80, 158, 190
Woodward, Andy 162
working time 151, 189
World Anti-Doping Agency 170, 174